Warman's®

U.S. COIN COLLECTING

EASY-TO-UNDERSTAND ADVICE FOR
BUYING & SELLING · STORAGE & CARE · GRADING

ALAN HERBERT

Published by

Krause Publications, a division of F+W Media, Inc.
700 East State Street • Iola, WI 54990-0001
715-445-2214 • 888-457-2873
www.shopnumismaster.com

To order books or other products call toll-free 1-800-258-0929
or visit us online at www.shopnumismaster.com

Library of Congress Control Number: 2010925145

ISBN-13: 978-1-4402-1368-7
ISBN-10: 1-4402-1368-2

Cover Design by Sharon Bartsch
Designed by Jana Tappa
Edited by Debbie Bradley

Printed in China

DEDICATION

To Joey Noyce, carrying on the collecting
tradition of his father, grandfather
and great-grandfather.

FOREWORD

When I started collecting coins in the 1970s, I was eager to gather as much information as I could. I subscribed to major numismatic publications, including *Coins* magazine, the one that first attracted my attention and that today I edit. I also followed advertisements and compiled 3-by-5-inch note cards on offerings in auction catalogs, jotting down, for later reference, the general strike characteristics and rarity levels of U.S. coins.

I was soon thoroughly immersed in the hobby. I knew the names of the major dealers and the major writers in the field. The problem was, I didn't know many fellow collectors. That is why, when the opportunity arose, I joined a local coin club and later the state collecting organization and ultimately the American Numismatic Association.

Along the way I've relished the opportunity to meet the hobby's top names and to learn from them. The book you are holding is by one of these true hobby luminaries. Alan Herbert's specialty has always been minting varieties. However, as an avid follower of everything he writes, I can tell you another real strong suit of his is in the area of common sense advice. Alan writes in an easy-to-read and understand fashion, and he explains topics thoroughly.

For instance, Alan reworked one of the hobby axioms into something clearer and more useful. Alan relates that you should "buy the book before you buy (or sell) the coin," which is an admonishment to new collectors to take care to learn the hobby before spending large sums of money on any tempting collectible, or before selling. As Alan often observes, you need to know as much to sell a coin as to buy one.

I'm amazed at the number of people who jump right in and buy coins or paper money without knowing a thing about what they are doing. So, like Alan says, you need to build a good reference library. But I would stress that you not only buy the book, but also that you read it. The more you learn the better equipped you'll be.

Coin collecting is a wonderful hobby. It allows anyone the chance to become an expert. Those who take advantage of this, and along the way follow the sage advice offered here by Alan Herbert on how to get started, how to handle and store coins, how to grade, etc., will find their enjoyment of the pastime greatly enhanced.

So read this book. It's a great hobby and there's no better teacher of the necessities in this regard than Alan Herbert.

Robert R. Van Ryzin
Editor, *Coins* magazine

TABLE OF CONTENTS

INTRODUCTION

First of all, let me warn you. If you have
picked this book in order to find out what
your coins are worth, you have the wrong
book. For values you need to consult a coin
price guide. This book is intended to get you
started collecting in the right direction with your coins, not how or where to buy
or sell them.

You probably already have noted the match between the cover of this book
and the Warman's coin folders. This is an important partnership that I will
explore with you in Chapter 12– Safekeeping your Coins.

The ancient Chinese described a part of the human head as "The Bump of
Curiosity." Yours is working, as demonstrated by the fact that you are curious
enough to open this book to see if coin collecting appeals to you.

Coin collecting is a hobby – one of the few that has something tangible to
show for the hours you put into it. However, it is also a thriving business for
the hundreds of coin dealers across the country. I happened to be one of the
fortunate few who turned coin collecting from a hobby into a full time job as a
journalist, which has carried me across the U.S. and to most of the countries in
Europe while affording me what amounts to a doctorate in coins. It gave me a
nickname – the AnswerMan – that stuck with me.

It's relatively easy to gather coins. Kept in a sock, an ashtray, a glass jar or
a milk can, coins get diverted from their regular task as money to a sedentary
life – until you come along and decide to make a collection out of these curious
pieces of metal. Just think, that 1793 large cent might have graced George
Washington's pocket, or bought something for Thomas Jefferson.

Collecting coins has unexpected benefits as you learn more about art,

economics, finance, history, geography and numerous other disciplines. It's impossible not to learn the many things that collecting offers. There are no limits beyond the scope of your imagination.

Further on you will find some rules, some "Do's" and "Don'ts." Everyone has rules and coin collecting is no different. We have unique signs and symbols – a secret language – that you can ignore for the time being. Ultimately, to round out your status as a serious collector, you will need to learn the language, which is awash with slang and nicknames. As you use the terms they will become more familiar to you.

If you are looking for a big quick profit, close this book carefully and put it back on the shelf. Coin collecting is primarily a hobby and investing is another matter completely. I never recommend coins as an investment for the beginning collector. You could also invest in sowbellies, but I don't recommend that for the beginning investor either.

Coin collecting is as diverse as you want to make it. Numismatics (pronounced NEW-mis-MAT-ics) covers coins, paper money, tokens, medals and other items used as money, or closely associated. Woodpecker scalps and bars of soap come to mind, among other unexpected objects used to buy or trade for things.

I mentioned rules, but really, one of the principal added attractions of coin collecting is that there are vast areas where there are no rules, other than any self-imposed checks and balances. For example, there is no rule that says you "have" to collect dog teeth. If you want to define any particular group of your coins as a "set," that's your call.

Other collectors may urge that you collect certain coins. You can cheerfully ignore them and go right ahead collecting your favorites. It's your choice and there are hundreds of ways to collect. You are free to collect what you like, what you enjoy and pieces that give you pride of ownership.

One important point, as you read on, is to make sure you are aware that I use "coin collecting" to cover coins, medals and tokens, to save having to repeat the whole definitions each time.

You will get advice on some things not to collect and there are quite a few "do's" and "don'ts" in this book. Perhaps the most important one in the whole book is: "Don't clean your coins." It's vitally important. The advice analogy I use is that I might tell you not to go to the beach and collect a bucket of sand, because it has zero value now and zero value later.

I will be happy to teach you as much as I can about this hobby, so read and enjoy. I've been writing about coin collecting, taking photos of coins and answering coin questions for nearly 50 years. My purpose in writing this book is to help you enjoy your hobby. A hobby is for fun, so read on.

Coins have been around for several thousand years. Methods of making coins as you can imagine have changed substantially over that period. Early examples

were crude, little more than lumps of metal with a punch mark or two. The transition to detailed figures came slowly. The secrets of enhancing coin production were lost and re-discovered.

Once the Medieval period (500-1500 C.E.) was over, the French introduced new methods that were a vast improvement. Early coin presses were crude, but an improvement over the hammered coins, which were made by placing a planchet on one die and hammering the other die to make an impression.

Hammered coins were gradually replaced with the invention of coin presses, which applied multiple tons of pressure to bring up the design. One key to their success was the thousands of identical coins that they could strike. Today's coin presses can spit out up to 750 coins per minute.

Making a coin is much like making nuts and bolts in large quantities. Although the minting process looks complicated, it is relatively simple when you consider it as three main items, the planchets, the dies and the strike. Back in 1972 I evolved the PDS Cataloging method using those three divisions, which has become a standard in the hobby.

Planchets are the material – usually a metal or alloy – upon which the coin is struck. The dies carry the design and apply the designs for both sides onto the planchet, making it a coin. Striking, as I've already noted, has progressed from the hammer to the high-speed coin press.

Planchets are made in a two-step process. Long strips of coin metal are run through blanking presses, which drive multiple blunt punches through the strip, punching as many as a dozen blanks from the strip at each stroke. This is a very noisy process and even though the blanking press is usually right on bedrock, it often shakes the building.

The blanks are passed through an upsetting mill, which turns the edge of the blank back creating a raised area of coin metal where the design rim will be on the struck coin. This upsetting turns the blank into a planchet. The two terms are often misused as a single term, "blank planchet," but the two are distinctly different stages.

The most common coin metal is copper while nickel, iron, zinc, silver and gold have all been used, usually in an alloy. Coin metals are chosen for a variety of factors, most especially availability and cost.

They must also produce an acceptable image with a minimum of wear on the dies. A die in most cases has the design incuse, or into the metal. You can learn for yourself what the die does by taking a piece of aluminum foil and pressing it against the design on a coin. When you remove the foil, the side next to the coin will be the same as a die, and the other side will have the design in relief as it appears on the hub, the tool used to make a die.

Most of today's dies are made by the hubbing method. The hub is a tool that has the design in relief, just as it appears on the coin. A master hub or master die is made by a machine that copies a plastic model, reducing it to the actual coin size and cutting it on the face of the hub or die.

The master die in turn is used to make working hubs by being pressed into a softened piece of tool steel. This is then hardened and used to make working dies by the same process, using a press that can exert hundreds of tons of pressure to form the design in the working die face. The transfer process is master hub to master die to working hub to working die. The master tools are never used to strike coins.

The process of striking coins, which began with the hammer, now is produced by a machine called a coin press. This is a machine that is capable of driving one die into the planchet with many tons of pressure. For example, a cent requires about 25 tons per square inch, while the old silver dollars needed 150 tons. The planchet is resting on, or is against the other die so when the strike occurs, both sides of the coin are formed at the same time. If the coin has a reeded edge, this is formed at the same time by a collar, often called the third die, which surrounds the planchet and has the reeding cut into the inside edge of the collar.

Remember that both sides and the edge are formed at the same time. You learned in physics class that you can't hold an object in mid-air and strike only one side. This is a point that many collectors flounder on.

It wouldn't hurt to re-read this description until you understand it. This is basic information about the minting process that every collector needs to know. As you progress you will want to learn more about the minting process. This is of special interest to those collecting minting varieties, but every collector needs to be familiar with the minting process, as the knowledge may save you from buying an altered or counterfeit coin.

You are going to find some statements or comments repeated. This is done intentionally, to underscore the importance of the comment or rule. Forgive me if it is advice you are already familiar with.

A final important point: There are about 70 world mints and most use the same equipment or methods, often from the same manufacturer, so some mishap that befalls a U.S. coin can usually be found on coins of other countries. I'll get into this a bit more in the chapter on World Coins.

CHAPTER 1

WHERE TO START

This chapter might also be titled "How to Start." There are many different paths to becoming a coin collector. You don't just wake up one morning and announce, "Today I will become a coin collector." Usually some particular event triggers curiosity, then interest and then the desire to get involved.

Beginning is as easy as putting a key in the ignition switch and starting a car. Look around you. There are coins everywhere – and don't ignore the paper money because there are many avid collectors who choose paper. In your dad's or grandad's pocket there are likely to be one or two state quarters.

Back in the early 1960s when I got interested in coins there were silver dimes, quarters and halves in circulation – and being close to Montana and Wyoming, I saw a lot of silver dollars. It was not unusual to see an Indian Head cent and there were plenty of Buffalo nickels. Today we find those state quarters and Lincoln cent commemoratives, as well as the Lewis and Clark nickels. Those three are called circulating commemorative coins, different from the usual commemoratives, which are made just for collectors.

Probably the most common path toward collecting involves your relatives. When Grandpa died he may have left a few coins in the drawer of his old roll top desk. Such a find carries with it the assumption that the coins may be valuable, or he wouldn't have stored them away.

Q:

In price charts I see IA and IB. What do they mean?

A:

Included Above and Included Below. While we are sometimes accused by irate readers of failing to include figures, the real reason is that there are no official figures available for a given date or mint. The same is true for many varieties, so the price guide has to lump two or more listings together to make any sense at all.

If Grandpa was a coin collector, there would be even more reason to expect the coins to have value. If you are lucky, he might have left behind a full-blown collection, replete with gold and silver pieces. The automatic urge at this point is: "Sell them! Take the money and run."

Whoa. Stop! Did you ever run a yard sale and agonize over what to charge because you had no idea of the real worth of the items? Do you know what to charge for the coins in his collection? In both cases the answer is "No," but that doesn't stop most heirs from accepting a fraction of what the coins might be worth. This is one of the most common mistakes made in coin collecting.

Before deciding what to do, take time to investigate. Hire an appraiser to tell you the value of the coins, which will be money well spent. Or, you can learn the values yourself by investing in a price guide and such other reference material as is needed. In the process you may decide to keep the coins, learn more about them and even add to the collection. Somewhere along this path you will realize that you have become a coin collector.

Does Dad always empty his pocket change into a bowl when he comes home from work? Most rabid collectors would consider that an accumulation, rather than a "true" collection. But remember, I said that you set the rules as to what you collect. Pocket change is less of a treasure trove than it was four or five decades ago, but you can still find state quarters, Lewis and Clark nickels and Lincoln commemorative cents buried among the common dates.

Many collectors started this way, with an accumulation of coins from some source. From that point, you are going to need knowledge in order to expand the group. This is perhaps the make or break point – whether to turn to some other collectible or spend money and time learning what you have and what you need to enhance or complete the group. I'm going to offer some advice and steer you through some of the pitfalls. This is the very beginning, and like other things in life, there are traps you need to avoid.

I can't solve every problem with a single book. I have seven overflowing bookcases of reference material. You probably won't need that many books, but with this as a starter you will learn what you need and add it to your bookshelf.

You are going to need to make room for a lot of new knowledge and dust off some little-used sections of your brain because there is a tremendous amount of available information for you to sort through. Perhaps "motivation" is the key word here. But, don't forget that there is fun involved in all this. A hobby is something to enjoy.

Already, you have questions. If you ask, you will be considered ignorant, stupid. Not so. Asking questions is the way to learn. One mantra you need to learn is: "There are no stupid questions."

"But you will laugh at me."

I am not going to laugh at you. Rather, I will

Q:
Where is gold found in the U.S.?

A:
21 states have commercial deposits; every state has at least traces.

Q:

What causes the difference in color in gold coins and gold jewelry?

A:

Pure gold is yellow. Copper makes it red, platinum makes it white, iron makes it green and bismuth will make it black. Green gold is defined as an alloy of 75 percent gold and 25 percent silver, but other ratios will also appear green, or a greenish tint.

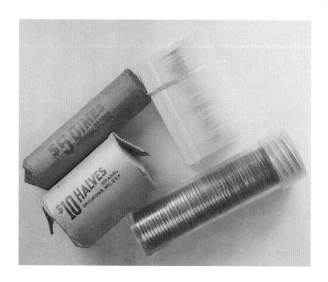

cheer you on for being curious enough to ask. I'm satisfied that if you ask, you are well on the way to becoming a coin collector.

The bigger your curiosity bump is, the faster you will progress as a collector because you will be learning things that ultimately will be of value to you. For example, learn not to be a checkbook or credit card collector. While buying your way into a collection is one of the few avenues left, it's pointless to waste money on coins that don't fit in your collecting interests. Many new collectors have a problem with this, wanting to buy everything in sight. Plan ahead, rather than buy ahead.

"But my question is one I'm sure you've answered before."

You are probably right, as new collectors as a group ask many of the same questions over and over. Some I've answered hundreds of times.

> *Ask, and keep asking. It's the road to success as a collector.*

Q:
What's the difference between gold leaf and gold foil?

A:
Gold leaf is thinner, only 1/200,000th of an inch thick, and nearly transparent. Gold foil varies in thickness to a minimum of 0.003 of an inch.

However, they frequently approach the question differently, so I learn from the questions. Ask, and keep asking. It's the road to success as a collector.

As you read through this book, you will find questions and answers, which are good examples of what collectors want to know. I answer questions in four of the F+W Media publications, and these are some of the common questions. I cover the spectrum, from novice to experienced collector, which is an enjoyable learning process for me as well.

As you get deeper into the hobby you will find that we experts don't always agree, but for the most part we stay calm. As but one example, I hate slang and nicknames but others freely use them in the hobby.

Coin collecting is not static. Price guides are effectively obsolete by the time they are printed, but many collectors foolishly think that a decades old price guide is all they need to evaluate their coins. Another problem is fads. Such things as premiums for unopened shipping boxes of mint and proof sets have taken their toll.

I've tried to insert at least one important message in each chapter, so it wouldn't hurt to keep this book handy and re-read it from time to time. I've tried to make it fun – for both of us. Much of this book is really an outline that you will eventually need to fill in from other sources.

Q:

Silver solder I know, but is there a gold solder?

A:

There is, and the formula is 12 parts of gold, two of silver and two of copper.

This is a good place to introduce mintmarks, as they play a vital role in coin collecting. Briefly, a mintmark is a letter or symbol on the coin that indicates the mint where it was struck. You'll find a more detailed explanation further on.

Do you know the difference between a coin, a token or a medal? Most people don't and the tendency is to lump all three as "coins." While they may look alike, there are some significant differences. Go to the glossary at the back of this book and you will see the three defined, which will help you realize the differences. The significance is that it is much harder to find reference material on tokens and medals than for coins.

An example of a medal from the 2010 American Numismatic Association convention

CHAPTER 2

WHAT IS MY COIN WORTH?

The most common question that I get asked in the mail and on the Internet is one that I can't answer: "What's it worth?" No one can answer it. Why not?

This is one question that no one can accurately answer for you. It's necessary to see the coin to determine its exact value. One important bit of advice is this: Let's assume that you acquire five or six State quarters. Your first question is going to be: "What are they worth?" Think about it. If they were really valuable, they probably wouldn't have wound up in your pocket, so follow this next rule: "Assume only face value until you've found out otherwise." Wishful thinking is not going to increase the value. It's tempting, but fruitless.

To answer the question, you need to forget for the moment that coins are made primarily for commerce used to pay for goods and services. There is a difference between face value and collector value. The most important difference is that collector value is not fixed. The simplest explanation is that just like a house or a car, you need to see it in order to determine the value.

Wear is a key factor. The more wear, the less the collector value. It's important enough to have a 70-point scale of wear. Assigning a number is defined as grading, a term you will hear frequently. Also important are the number minted and in some cases the estimated survivors. Sometimes, it even depends on the rarity of a specific grade.

A common request is to provide a price range. That's something I won't

By base silver does
one mean a low-grade
silver alloy?

A:
That's the generally
accepted numismatic
meaning. It is the
same thing as billon,
an alloy containing
less than 50 percent
silver. Black billon is an
alloy of 75% copper
and 25% silver, noted
for tarnishing to an
ugly blackish color at
a moment's notice.

do either, because for most people a range is
meaningless and perhaps unexpectedly creates a
serious problem. As an example, a 1903 Barber dime
catalogs at $4 in the lowest grade and $1,100 in the
highest grade. If I quote that range to a collector he
will automatically assume that his battered and bent
coin is worth $1,100. That's human nature.

If a dealer offers anything less, the customer
stomps out, convinced the dealer is ripping him off.
The coin business is the only one I'm aware of where
the majority of customers expect full retail for their
coins, not wanting to understand that a dealer has to
have a profit margin to stay in business.

The solution is to learn how to grade your coins
yourself, a topic covered in the "Grading Your Coins"
chapter.

**"Know more about the coin you are buying than
does the person selling it."**

That applies to grading as much, or even more,
than other factors. As you gain experience, the figures
in a price guide will have more meaning for you. A
vital point here is that there are two kinds of catalogs,
with a lot of confusion about them. A price guide is
a reference catalog, not an offer to buy or sell. These
prices are average retail prices and they are not set in
stone. The coin dealers use the quotes as a starting
point to which they apply their personal formula, so
you may never see a dealer's prices that exactly match
the price guide

Every price guide clearly states that it is not a sale
catalog and that the publisher does not buy or sell

coins. If you are unsure of what a given catalog is, look for an order blank. If you don't find one, you can be reasonably sure it's a reference catalog.

A catalog that offers coins for sale or offers to buy coins is a sales catalog and the prices quoted are actual sell or buy prices. The text will clearly indicate which type of catalog it is.

One misconception is that just because a coin is listed in a price guide, there is a market for it. The fact is that since anyone can search coins, there is a surplus of low-value coins, far more than any market for them. Coin values are like any other commodity. If there's a shortage, the price and demand goes up. If there's a surplus, the demand is met and the price goes down.

If there's a library within a reasonable distance, go to it and ask for their reference section. Find a coin price guide and compare your coins. At this point you will see the term "grade" used. I've devoted a chapter to grading, but for the moment, when you see a range of values take one of the lowest figures rather than the highest as the likely value of your coin.

In 99 out of 100 cases, the price guide is going to confirm your assumption of value. Still, you have the makings of a collection, what with quarters from 50 states and the six extras for the District of Columbia and U.S. Territories. As you leaf through you will find recent dollar coins you may never have seen, as well as other coins that capture your interest.

Larger bookstores carry price guides or you can order them on the Internet. Check out the price guides at www.shopnumismaster.com. Your local

Q:
How many of the old large cents were there to a "cask?"

A:
After 1795 the weight of the cent figured out to 41 2/3 coins to an avoirdupois pound. A cask held 336 pounds, or 14,000 large cents.

Q:

Why did they use silver in the wartime nickels during World War II?

A:

The principal reason was an effort to save both copper and nickel that were in short supply and urgently needed for a variety of wartime needs. A major factor in selecting silver was the fact that – for the government at least – it was both plentiful and cheap.

coin dealer also is likely to have copies for sale.

"Walk before you run!" Put your checkbook away, and then keep looking. Establish a budget for your collection, including reference material to add to your library. Avoid big ticket coins until you have lots of experience, as there are many pitfalls. Pick coins that you can afford, as a mistake here could easily sour you on further coin collecting.

One of the major changes in the hobby has been the shift in collector interest. Just about every collector over the age of 50 started by collecting cents. State quarters rank first now, followed by silver dollars (Morgan and Peace dollars). Cents are down to third or fourth, but may be coming back up with the Lincoln commemoratives of 2009. Cents are a good place to start and your next step will be to get an album or folder. Filling the holes is a good way to start your collection. *By the way, they are not "pennies." The British have pennies and pence, but we have cents. It says so right on the coin.*

This is also a good time to get to know your local coin dealer. He has the folders and other storage materials and can offer sage advice and answer your questions. Learn to shut up when he is waiting on another customer and don't walk out without buying something. Regular customers usually get better treatment. I'll discuss coin dealers more in a separate chapter.

Once you've dug under the sofa cushions and a few other typical hiding places, it's time to expand your horizons. Church collection plates used to be a prime source for coins, but today most donations are notes or checks. If you or your family has an account at a local bank, this may work to your advantage. Banks carry rolls or even bags of coins. You can get a roll or two at face, but you may be able to get larger quantities to search if you agree to pay the shipping charges that banks are charged by the Federal Reserve Bank.

One other possible source is city hall – they get lots of foreign coins in the parking meters. A jukebox operator or an arcade are both likely to have a small bucket of tokens and odd coins. A casino will sell you quarters if they still use them. Most have gone to a paper receipt system so that source is drying up. Self-service car washes usually have a quarter slot.

When dealing with banks, learn their rules. You may have to write your name or phone number on rolls you return. It's not cool to replace coins with washers.

Time to repeat a very important rule: "Buy the book before you buy (or sell) the coin."

Think about this advice and then follow it. The collector who spends all his money on coins and neglects his reference library is asking for trouble. Also, you need to know as much to sell a coin as you do to buy a coin.

And, a second piece of advice is repeated: "Know more about the coin than does the person selling it to you."

If you're doing business with a 30-year veteran coin dealer this is difficult, but do the research

Q:
If an object, such as a pattern coin, is "gilded" does that mean it is gold plated?

A:
Gilding may mean either plated with gold or with some material (such as bronze powder) that simulates or resembles the appearance of gold. In most cases gilding on pattern coins is something other than gold, as gold plated pieces usually are described as plated.

What authority did
President Franklin
D. Roosevelt have
to close the banks,
prohibit the sale or
export of gold and
stop the minting of
U.S. gold coins in 1933?

A:

None, very little or
lots depending on
who you talked to at
the time. Authorities
on Constitutional law
claimed that there
was little if any legal
precedent for his
actions and that they
were quite probably
unconstitutional.

anyway. You might just learn something the dealer has forgotten. This is an incentive to do some thorough research before buying a particular coin.

Once you've learned to leave your checkbook and credit card at home, you're ready to do some serious collecting. Add to your collection slowly, savoring each new addition. Study it. Research it. Learn to grade it yourself. Assert your pride of ownership, but don't broadcast the fact that you are a coin collector. Burglars assume that anyone with two coins to rub together is rich in potential loot.

Back to an inherited collection for a moment; I preach patience. If the coins are properly stored they will hold their value and even become worth more. As you learn more about them you will better understand what needs to be done with them. The key word is properly stored, a topic I'll get into further on.

Learning how to handle your coins is of vital importance. A fingerprint can ruin a valuable coin. The topic is important enough to devote a chapter to it further on. Read it before you touch a proof or uncirculated coin.

If you already have a collection started I urge you to read this book from cover to cover to avoid some of the common pitfalls. The same goes for you and your accumulation or collection. Proper care will pay for itself a hundred times over.

CHAPTER 3

What you

See...

When you look at a coin, the first thing you usually see is the central design: a bust, a building or some other object. Now that you are looking at coins as something to collect rather than spend, there are some important things for you to do, to develop a routine to use as you look at larger numbers of coins.

First, look at the design. Then look at the date and finally the mintmark. Look at all the elements of the obverse design. Then turn the coin over and look at all the elements of the reverse design. Look for obvious damage and telltale signs that the coin has been cleaned or doctored. Check the edge for problems. It's very important that you use this routine on each coin to avoid missing problems or damage, or with luck, finding a minting variety.

Set aside any coin that has something different for a detailed examination later. Avoid the temptation to glance at the date and go on to the next coin. At first you are likely to have a fairly large pile of those "different" coins. As you gain knowledge the pile will shrink. As you go back through you may not even be able to remember why you set some coins aside, but that's part of the learning process.

Another important rule: "Don't depend on the naked eye."

Always use a magnifier when looking at coins. A low power is fine

Q:

I'm told that the Chinese laborers in the California gold fields were more interested in silver than in gold. Is this correct?

A:

Silver was much more popular as a matter of tradition and availability, and accounts of the gold rush indicate that the laborers paid in gold dust would quickly trade it for silver coins.

for large numbers, but you need at least a 10X magnifier to look at something unusual.

The more coins you look at, the easier it will be to spot the defects or tell tale signs of a counterfeit or altered coin. With a little practice you can develop a photographic memory that will alert you when there is something "wrong" with the coin you are looking at.

"First, make a list."

This is advice that can be repeated and repeated because it is so important. For the heir faced with an inherited collection or the novice collector, a list is vital. This is the foundation of your collection. Put down the denomination, the date and the mintmark, three items that are invaluable to the collector. With a list in hand along with some representative coins, you can shop your collection to several dealers without having to drag the entire collection from store to store. The IRS will want a copy too.

"Don't broadcast that you are a coin collector."

A little bragging before the wrong ears can set you up for an unwelcome visitor. Stress to family members and friends that your collection not be discussed in public places. You can assert your pride of ownership without endangering your collection. Burglars are alert to any indication of potential value.

CHAPTER 4

Handling Your
COINS

At first you may be skeptical of the information in this chapter, but it's advice that will stay with you as long as you collect.

We all are used to handling coins. You pull out a handful and spend them or pay for something and put the rest of them back in your pocket or purse. How did you hold the coins you selected?

Guess what. You made one of the most common of mistakes in handling coins for a collection. You held the coin between your thumb and finger, pressed on the front and back of the coin – what collectors call the obverse and reverse of the coin.

Holding a coin like that is not a problem with coins that show wear, but for an uncirculated or proof coin you just damaged the coin because the natural oils in your skin will etch a fingerprint or a thumb print into the surface of the coin in a matter of minutes. Once the fingerprint is on the coin it's impossible to remove without further damaging the coin.

"Always hold a coin by the edge, never the faces."

It's a good habit to get into. If you are working with upper-grade, uncirculated or proof coins, a pair of lintless cotton gloves is strongly recommended. Latex or plastic gloves are not recommended because they often have powder or lubricants on them that may damage the coin.

Family or friends may want to touch the coins. You have a couple of

"Always hold a coin by the edge, never the faces."

choices. You can either yell at them, or warn them not to touch the coins, or show them how to correctly handle them. Or put the coins in holders that protect the surface of the coin. Heaven forbid they drop one of your coins.

Many an old-time collector or dealer will use the "ring" test to determine if a coin is silver. Unfortunately, besides being a negative test, it potentially damages the coin since it involves dropping the coin on a hard surface. It's a negative test, because the slightest fissure or internal crack in the coin will make it sound like a lead washer. Weighing the coin will tell you as much or more about the coin and weighing is a non-destructive test. Don't let someone else "ring" your coin, either.

"Don't scratch, cut, clean, rub or polish a coin for any reason."

For instance, it's impossible to cut through copper plating, as the metal curls around the blade, giving you the false impression that the coin is solid copper. Stop anyone else from "testing" your coin in this fashion as the damage done will often cut the collector value of the coin in half, or worse. Weighing the coin will tell you a lot more, and as I said, it's a non-destructive test.

The whole idea behind this is to protect the mint-produced surface. The more wear or damage there is to the coin's surface, the less it is going to be worth. The whole basis of collecting coins revolves around protecting and preserving that mint surface. I'll expand on this theme in the next chapter.

CHAPTER 5

DON'T
CLEAN
YOUR COINS!

This is a good place to repeat, "Don't clean your coins."

If you don't learn anything else from this book, this rule will save you many times the cover price.

There are two types of cleaning, often confused with each other.

Destructive cleaning uses abrasives or acids to clean (and alter) the coin surfaces. Non-destructive cleaning uses solvents that are harmless to the coin metal.

Destructive cleaning will reduce the collector value as much as 50 percent or even more. An expert can, in some cases, improve the coin value by cleaning, but for the average collector the risk of damage is too great, as almost anything you do is going to cut the value. Unless you are an experienced specialist, the "don't clean" rule stands. The typical response from people who don't take advice kindly is "I'll do as I please with my coins and you can go jump in the lake!" Have a nice swim.

If you are one of those, then don't waste time reading any further, but your heirs are not going to appreciate your independence. I know of one collector who had thousands of silver dollars. Every coin had been scrubbed with a harsh abrasive and every coin he bought got the same treatment, despite dire warnings from friends and dealers he did business with. The

DEFINITION:

A flip is a small PVC, Mylar, or plastic pocket that folds in half and is designed to hold one coin. Flips usually measure 2 inches square (when folded), but they also come in 1.5-inch and 2.5-inch sizes.

result – the only value left was the silver content, less than an ounce in each coin.

Another collector put his coins through a rock tumbler, ruining the collector value. I had the task of telling him his entire collection of several thousand coins was worthless to collectors after he flew half way across the country to where I lived and rented a motel room to show them to me.

The metal cleaners you see offered for sale on TV and elsewhere all are acid-based cleaners that remove some of the surface metal in the process of cleaning a coin. These are to be avoided. On the other hand, a weak soap (not detergent) solution in distilled water will remove dirt and grease from an encrusted coin without damaging it.

City tap water has chlorine in it, which will discolor the coin. Use distilled water and rinse with distilled water. Acetone is another commonly used solvent, but there is a fire hazard that you should be aware of. Fingernail polish remover contains acetone, but it has other chemicals that may cause damage to upper grade coins.

Also this warning: There is no safe method available to clean your upper grade uncirculated or proof coins or copper alloy coins.

After using solvents, it's important to rinse the coins with distilled water and then either allow them to air dry, or pat them dry. Never rub, even with the softest cloth.

Heavily encrusted coins can be soaked for several months in olive oil. The oil won't damage the coin further, but it will eventually dissolve the

"Don't buy a cleaned coin unless it is absolutely the last resort."
Cleaned coins will show little or no appreciation, lagging far
behind an uncleaned version of the same coin.

crust. Trying to restore badly corroded coins is a waste of time. Even if you successfully remove the corrosion, there is permanent damage underneath, leaving you with a near worthless coin. The same applies to the patina on ancient coins. Don't buy coins that have been cleaned. The bargain prices indicate the coins will not appreciate as quickly as coins left uncleaned.

Anywhere else, the discoloration on silver is called tarnish, but coin collectors blithely refer to it as "toning." It can range from black to many of the rainbow colors and some collectors will pay a premium for nice looking toning. This comes close to being a fad. It is also subject to abuse from artificial toning.

An ultrasound cleaner will work, but with care. Only one coin at a time should be cleaned and the solution in the bowl should be changed frequently.

Another threat to your coins is PVC (polyvinyl chloride). It is a softener used in plastics, such as the 2-x-2 coin flips. When it deteriorates, from age or excessive heat, it creates a green slime that will eat into the surface of the coin, doing irreversible and permanent damage to the coin. There are Mylar flips available which do not have this problem.

"Don't buy a cleaned coin unless it is absolutely the last resort."

Cleaned coins will show little or no appreciation, lagging far behind an uncleaned version of the same coin.

CHAPTER 6

TOOLS
OF THE TRADE

No matter what the job, you will probably need tools and other equipment to get the job done. Coin collecting is no different. It's much easier and more fun if you have the right tools. I've already mentioned magnifiers, but some repetition is not going to hurt.

A magnifier is rated by the increase in size of the image. A 1-power magnifier will show you a correctly sized image. A 10X magnifier will show the image 10 times larger than normal. "X" in this case means "times."

"EVERY coin collector needs at least one magnifier."

You should never examine a coin just with the unaided eye, whether buying or selling. The mark of the experienced collector is the magnifier hanging from a lanyard around his neck.

Magnifiers come with glass or plastic lenses. It's quite worthwhile to spend the extra money on glass as a good lens will last you a lifetime. I use a 14X lens that I bought in 1967 and there is not a scratch on the lens, despite a dozen trips to the floor.

As a collector, you need a low power lens for looking at multiple coins, plus a stronger lens to investigate something you spotted. A low power usually lets you see all of the coin, while a higher powered one may only show you something the size of the date.

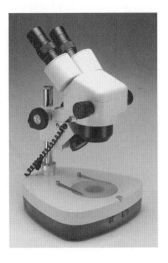

Obviously, a lens allows you to see more. That extra viewing power comes in handy when you suspect a coin of being a counterfeit, or an altered or doctored coin. The more coins you look at – and really see – the easier it will be to spot the problem coins. Over the years I've seen hundreds of coins that appear bright and shiny to the unaided eye, but under magnification reveal that they have been buffed or polished or even sand blasted to create that bright finish.

I have done a lot of authentication work in the past and I was fortunate enough to have a stereo microscope given to me. This turned out to be invaluable in my work and I took thousands of pictures through it. If you have access to a microscope, it becomes an indispensable tool for authentication or research work. If you have some cash available, a good stereo microscope will cost a minimum of $300.

For coins you need a stereo model with a 20X to 40X range. Anything over that, such as the 1200X scopes commonly found in schools, is overkill and useless for coins. With 60X you can find something "wrong" with almost every coin.

When using a strong hand lens or a microscope, turn and tilt the coin to get the light from different angles. This will expose such common problems as light, or reflection doubling, caused by the light bouncing off a shiny coin. It will also help you catch defects, doctoring or maybe even some hub doubling, which in some instances can increase the value of a coin. More on that later on.

A handy trick for your microscope is to invert a plastic cup with a flat bottom

Q:

Are there any "blue laws" still on the books relating to coins?

A:

Probably not too many, although the State of New Hampshire didn't get around to repealing one coinage legal matter until 1950. The repealed item was a clause in the State Constitution which required that money matters were to be computed in shillings and pence.

and put the coin on that. It allows you to turn the coin without touching it, cutting the handling down to a minimum.

Another handy tool that will safely handle coins is a pair of plastic coin tongs. They are made with jaws that contact a minimum of the edge of the coin so they are quite safe to use.

A must for the serious collector is a scale. Weighing a coin will tell you far more than cutting or scratching it. I have two scales. One is a Redding gunpowder scale, which uses grains rather than ounces, from 500 down to 1/10th of a grain, which is plenty for coins. They are available from any dealer who has reloading equipment for sale. The other is an Ohaus balance scale that is even more accurate and has provisions for running specific gravity tests – another research tool. Between the two scales I can solve many of the coin problems that come across my desk. There are also electronic scales that will fit in your shirt pocket, invaluable at a coin show.

You should make it a practice to weigh each coin before adding it to your collection. It will easily catch some of the more flagrant counterfeit coins.

The odds are that you already have a computer, so this would not be an added expense. There is very usable software available to catalog your collection and some even will connect to a pricing source. If you have a digital camera you can store copies of your coins.

If you prefer not to get software for these tasks, you can always use the word processor you already

Some dealers seem to make a game of seeing how close they can come to the coin with the staples, a dangerous game you don't want to play.

have, as that has search capabilities that make it easy to use. I have been using WordPerfect software for this purpose for nearly three decades.

A good heavy-duty stapler is a must, You will be doing a lot of stapling on cardboard 2x2 holders and it takes some force to drive the staple through two layers. I have one that came from a government surplus sale that has served faithfully for many years.

"Keep staples as far away as possible from the coin."

You will also need a pair of needle nose pliers to flatten the legs of the staples, to avoid damage to other coins. Some dealers seem to make a game of seeing how close they can come to the coin with the staples, a dangerous game you don't want to play. The staples are a threat and the overhang of the stapler may damage the coin.

An inexpensive protractor is useful, especially when you find a coin with the reverse rotated out of its normal position.

Don't forget a good light. Highly recommended is one of the goose-neck or swing-arm lamps that clamp on the edge of a table or desk and that you see at every coin show. For nearly all work a 60-watt bulb will do the trick, but some may prefer a 100-watt, especially for photography.

There are also halogen lights that are useful. Some photographers prefer them, but the regular incandescent bulbs will do the job. One warning, avoid florescent lights, as they tend to distort what you see on the coin.

Metal detectors are often touted as a coin collecting tool but the unfortunate fact is that nearly all the coins recovered with detectors are corroded to the point of being valueless to the collector. I can cite examples of collectible coins, but they are definitely a minority.

CHAPTER 7

YOUR COLLECTION AND THE LAW

The IRS has an interest in your collection. If you buy or sell coins, it wants to see the supporting paperwork against the day you retire from collecting and sell your collection. The rules are somewhat complicated, so if you get deeper into collecting, or become a coin dealer, you will need to consult a tax service.

The IRS requires records to support purchases and sales. If you can't prove what you paid for a given coin that you sell, it can assess any amount above the face value as profit. If you received coins as a gift, it's a good idea to establish a value at the time you received them by checking price guides for the period.

The sooner you start, the fewer problems you will have in finding price records. The better your records, the less likely you are to get audited. This applies to other collectibles as well. In some instances, the IRS may require an appraisal by a recognized appraiser.

Without an inventory, your heirs or the executor of your estate will have no clue as to what the coins are and what they are worth. In numerous cases, estate coins are sold for a fraction of their actual value because of this lack of knowledge. Leave specific instructions as to how to dispose of the coins in the collection in your will. This is especially true for minting varieties, which require a specialist dealer to handle them.

If you have a specialty collection, whether minting varieties, Roman coins or

> *If you received coins as a gift, it's a good idea to establish a value at the time you received them by checking price guides for the period.*

tokens, make sure that your list includes the name and contact information for one or more dealers that you would recommend or that you have done business with. It's not a bad idea to make advance arrangements with your dealer of choice, so that they will be aware of what's coming and will be prepared to handle it.

It's also an excellent idea to make a specific bequest of your collection, either to your estate if there isn't an individual heir who would like to continue it, or to some group that would give your estate a tax benefit, such as the American Numismatic Association in Colorado Springs, Co.

It is usually a bad idea to gift an organization that is not involved with coins or bequeath a collection to several non-collectors, which mandates a sale to divide the assets. One of the most common complaints I get from collectors is that there is no one else in the family who has the slightest interest in coin collecting. I'm fortunate enough to have a great-grandson, Joey Noyce, who is an avid collector.

Also, if you have an inventory it can be of substantial value if your house burns down or is burglarized. List the denomination, date, mintmark and approximate grade. If you have it on your computer, be sure you have a backup copy.

I recommend getting rid of any counterfeit coins that you come across. It is illegal to possess, buy or sell them. Turn them in to your bank or a local Secret Service office.

CHAPTER 8

THE
INTERNET

As a collector you are likely to turn to the Internet for any of a variety of reasons. While the Web can be of significant help, it's very important that you recognize it, and your, limitations.

A mandatory rule, especially for the novice collector, is to avoid buying any coins on the Internet, at least until you have a thorough grounding in grading. The rule to follow here is:

"Don't buy a coin without seeing it, until you can grade it yourself."

Learning to grade any coin accurately is a talent that will save you many dollars over a lifetime of collecting. Don't depend on others to do your grading for you.

On the bright side, the Internet is a limitless source of free information. Learn to use any of the search engines to answer your questions. For a typical research project that I did recently, the search engine listed 500,000 pages of information. The most important information, however, was on the very first page, as is usually the case.

There are several price guides posted on the net, but I recommend the following:

— F+W Media NumisMaster site at www.numismaster.com.

— For all of the Krause numismatic publications and catalogs
go to: www.shopnumismaster.com

Unfortunately, not all the information found on the Internet is correct. If you have the slightest doubt, be sure to confirm the information from another source.

It has been quite interesting to see the mass exodus to the Internet. In a matter of a year or two it has gone from mention in one or two ads in a typical magazine listing a website to the point where almost every advertisement includes a web address.

CHAPTER 9

WHAT SHOULD I
BID?

The average person is likely to be more familiar with coin auctions on the Internet, but there is much more going on than that. Several large auction houses only do coin auctions and hundreds of country auctions disperse large quantities of coins. There are also firms that only do telephone or mail bid auctions.

The major coin auction firms issue catalogs for the sales they conduct, as well as setting up a room where the lots can be examined by potential bidders.

Most coin auction catalogs contain a wealth of information that is not always available from other sources. The photos are of the actual coins in the auction, a point that is not always true of coins offered on the Internet.

A typical sale may contain up to several thousand lots. A lot may consist of a single coin, or it may contain several hundred coins as there usually is no limit on lot size. If you have your eye on a single coin in a lot with multiple coins, you must bid on the entire lot, not try to separate the coin from the rest of the lot.

There are other well established rules that are pretty much standard for coin auctions usually stated in clear language in the sale catalog. It is well worth the time spent reading the rules and getting familiar with them, so that you don't unintentionally break them, to your embarrassment.

A steadily growing trend for such auctions is to charge both the seller and the buyer a fee, making up part of the profit for the auction firm. These fees get into double digit percentages so it's important to consider them when bidding on a lot.

There are numerous forms of auctions, both public and private. Most coin auctions are public, allowing anyone to bid. You may never hear of a private auction, held behind closed doors and by invitation only. Another term is "private treaty." This is essentially an agreement between two parties to sell the coin at an agreed on price.

Bidding at a coin auction is much like other auctions. There is usually a reserve price which must be met to satisfy the consignor. The bidders

Q:
I have an 1804 dollar that must be quite valuable from what I read about it. How do I go about selling it?

A:
The last genuine Class I 1804 dollar, one of those made by the Mint in 1834-35, turned up in 1962 in what is now known as the King of Siam proof set. The chances of your coin being genuine, regardless of whatever history you may have for it, range from slim to none.

> *It's not uncommon to see coins bid up to two or three times their actual value.*

may be in the room, have mailed in their bids or are using the telephone or Internet to place their bids.

The auction houses usually charge for the catalogs to defray part of the expense. Page after page of color photos don't come cheap. A search through a used bookstore usually will turn up a wide assortment of inexpensive auction catalogs, in themselves collectible. A handful of book dealers also handle them and feature them – especially the big "name" sales – in their catalogs or auctions. Many auction catalogs are devoted to coins from a single collector, usually one prominent in the hobby.

The auction houses also use the Internet to display important lots from a forthcoming sale. This allows them to reach a much wider selection of potential bidders. They are worth a look to further your hobby education (search: "coin auctions").

Country auctions, while interesting, are not recommended as a place to buy coins. Except in rare cases the auctioneer has only a basic knowledge of coins and their values. The big negative factor is that the public doesn't have any knowledge either and they tend in many cases to overbid the coins being offered, paying much more than they are worth. It's not uncommon to see coins bid up to two or three times their actual value. Silver dollars are likely to go for even more. The sellers of course are tickled to death with that kind of bidding.

Many local coin clubs offer regular auctions as part of, or next to the club meetings. They may also in some cases offer members a mail bid sale. The American Numismatic Association (www.money.org) has major auctions at its annual shows.

CHAPTER 10

Sellers
BEWARE

All of us have seen the flamboyant TV ads and hucksters, the ads in service organization magazines and the full page newspaper ads from "motel room operators" offering to pay top dollar for your coins.

"In general, if the company doesn't advertise in the hobby press, take your business elsewhere."

TV, radio and newspaper ads are mostly uncontrolled, so they can say just about anything, or skirt the truth. These firms use a team of lawyers to keep their ads as close to the edge as possible. The hobby publications usually weed out such ads since they are a detriment to the hobby.

When you see an ad from one of the firms that sets up shop typically in a motel or hotel room, you'll see the line: "We pay up to...." for a certain coin. It should immediately raise a red flag. Over the years I have been told of numerous incidents, such as an elderly lady being offered face value for her gold coins. In a recent case, the buyer was deducting a 25 percent "smelting fee." The sad part is that if these people had taken the coins to an established local coin dealer they would have undoubtedly gotten much more for their coins. Borderline ads are deliberately targeted toward the uninformed. Their favorite target is the proverbial "little old lady in tennis shoes."

TV and newspaper ads don't come cheap. You know that if a firm is paying heavily for their ads, the profit has to come from somewhere, such as out of your pocket.

Mixed in with ads offering gold for sale are offers of "coins" cunningly couched to obliterate the fact that they are not coins, and that their "gold filled" pieces contain only a minute amount of gold, just enough to plate the piece. Gold plating was prohibited for many years. So, when that law was repealed companies fell over each other in a rush to offer real coins that had been gold plated.

The public is taken in by the fact that some of the pieces are legitimate coins, so they pay a healthy premium for what amounts to altered coins, which probably never will appreciate. Privately minted copies of real coins often are correctly labeled as "non monetary," but it's a term easily misunderstood. Simply put, it's not money, so it's not a coin.

One of the gold advertisements brag that gold "never has been worth zero." Like many other misleading statements this is incorrect. When gold was first discovered it had no value until someone found that they could make jewelry out of it. The same applies to the statement that "Gold does not go down, it goes up."

Another ad offers the "Last 4,000" Morgan dollars, ignoring the fact that there are an estimated 300 million of them still around. Avoid firms that have to run disclaimers that their sound-alike names are not affiliated with the official United States Mint.

"Beware of telemarketers offering coins for sale."

The sight unseen rule covers this, so I'd urge you never to buy coins over the phone from someone you don't know who called you. However, if you have done business with the firm, they may call you with impunity. I've seen many collections of telemarketer coins that are worth only a fraction of the thousands of dollars the victims paid for them. Surprisingly, the targets were doctors, lawyers and other professional people who should have known better.

"Be careful of anyone who labels a token or medal as a coin."

This is out and out misleading advertising, as only a government can issue a coin. See the definitions in the glossary to learn the difference. The monetary difference can be significant as coins are well cataloged while reference material for medals and tokens is limited. There are only a relative handful of rare and valuable medals, far outnumbered by rare coins with known mintages.

Certificates of Authenticity are as worthless as the paper they are printed on. They are not affixed to a coin, so they can be moved from coin to coin without recourse. Any ad that touts a certificate as a selling point is suspect. Unfortunately it has become a fad and even the official mints are including them with their collector coins. Coins that have been graded by third party grading services carry their pedigree with them, as they are sealed in hard plastic holders, called "slabs."

Always read the fine print on any paperwork. Make sure you fully understand the terms and don't assume anything, or accept a verbal promise. Ask questions until you are fully satisfied and then proceed with caution. Above all, get it in writing. Don't accept verbal promises.

Coins or medals are being altered with enameled designs. The Royal Canadian Mint is one of several mints offering genuine colorized coins, but the jury is still out on whether they will appreciate in value.

Relatives and friends of collectors are often the unwitting dupes. They go out and buy colorfully packaged coins for gifts, more often than not buying coins that the collector has, or buying coins that have been cleaned, altered or damaged, worthless to the collector. If you must buy a gift for a collector, a gift certificate from his coin dealer will solve the problem.

You comparison shop for other items, so why not coins? The odds are that you can match or beat any of these motel room dealer's offers by patronizing your local coin dealer. You can often beat the price by a third or a half.

CHAPTER 11

BUYING
& SELLING

There are some very important rules and regulations that apply to buying or selling, some unique to the coin hobby. The key rule has to do with those 2x2 cardboard holders and sealed plastic holders.

"If you buy a coin in a holder and remove it, by removing the staples or breaking the seal, the coin is yours."

This means that you cannot legally return the coin for a refund if you discover it has been cleaned or has some other problem.

Opening the holder, without specific written permission from the seller voids any guarantee or return privileges. This is for the dealer's protection, so the rule is rigidly enforced. Obviously, you need to be very careful until you are satisfied that the coin is as represented. A simple solution is to ask the dealer to open the holder, so that you can examine the coin before buying it.

This rule causes problems if you send the coin in to be graded, as the examiner will have to open the holder in order to examine the coin. This is where seller permission is required, because otherwise he would have legal grounds to void his guarantee. The best way to avoid this is to ask the dealer to send the coin in for grading before you buy it.

If you are selling coins to a dealer, or having a collection appraised or graded there is often concern that they might switch coins and substitute a lesser grade coin. This is unlikely to happen. There is no 100 percent guarantee, but since their reputation keeps them in business there are very few instances of switching.

It might surprise you that for every dealer who risks his reputation there are a hundred collectors doing their best to scam the dealer, so in most cases it is your fellow collector that you need to watch. Talk to any coin dealer and they can reel off hundreds of stories of sellers trying to trick them.

One problem for dealers is the collector who comes in and says "I'm a dealer, so I want a discount." A couple of quick questions will reveal that he is not a dealer and doesn't rate discounts that apply in dealer-to-dealer transactions. Dealers will give discounts for a variety of reasons, especially if a customer buys several coins or a more expensive coin but they are in business to make a living, not to give away money.

If you are buying, make a list of the coins you are looking for with prices for the grade you have in mind. When you see a coin you want, you have the list to compare with the dealer's price. There are no fire sale prices for coins, so be wary of any serious markdowns. That's where your list comes in handy again and again.

In many cases, it is important to buy the big ticket coins you need for your collection first, then get the less expensive dates or mints later. This applies in most cases because the more

Q:
Do books on coins affect the market?

A:
There is a very definite correlation between the publishing of a book on the hobby, especially one that offers prices, or covers some specialized area. This is likely to be even truer if the book covers some phase that hasn't been covered before. The best advice—buy the book before you buy or sell the coin.

expensive coins or grades are likely to increase in value faster than the more common dates. Most collectors start with the cheaper coins, only to find that the expensive ones are priced out of sight by the time they get to them. As a beginner, you should take it slowly, as you can get burned more on a valuable coin than on an inexpensive one.

Here's where you get to put what you've learned from this book on the line:

1. Buy the book before you buy – or sell – the coin.

2. Know more about the coin than does the person selling it.

3. Know how to grade within a point.

4. Keep accurate records of every purchase and sale. The IRS is waiting.

5. Learn the minting process.

6. Collect what you like and want, not what someone tells you to collect.

7. There are no dumb questions.

8. Don't clean your coins.

9. Walk before you run.

10. Make a list.

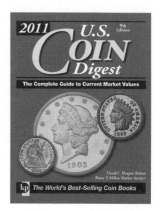

CHAPTER 12

SAFEKEEPING YOUR
COINS

One of your early concerns as a collector is the safe storage and protection of your collection. Storage methods vary widely and there are numerous potential hazards that could damage or even destroy your favorite collectible.

The two topics fit together as some of the things you do to store your coins and some of the hazards go together. Some you can insure against, others you can't, and it's frequently impossible to replace valued pieces in your collection.

Coins need to be protected from handling and from pollution or contamination in the air around us. Add in the possibilities of a fire or a flood, or a broken waterline in your house. There are burglars and home invasion baddies that will strip your collection to the bone. Some of these security things you will want to do yourself. Some of you are probably going to have to risk it because of the expense factor. When your collection gets into the triple digits it's time to find a safety deposit box at a bank.

Before you sign up, read the fine print in the box contract. If the vault is broken into, the bank's insurance may not cover the loss. Homeowner's Insurance probably won't cover it either, but you can buy a special policy that will protect your collection at home, or in the bank. Usually there is a discount for coins kept in the bank. Talk to your insurance agent.

Q:
Why is the low mintage 1931-S cent only valued at $163 in MS-60? As a new collector I'm puzzled by the inconsistency.

A:
The chief reason is that collectors jumped on the coin as soon as it was released and large quantities were saved in original rolls. Even after it was determined to be a low mintage coin, they could still be purchased over the counter from the Mint. Few of the coins circulated, hence the flat price curve for the circulated grades.

Coins are much like humans. They like the same moderate temperatures and low humidity that we like. That's why the attic and the basement are ruled out as places to keep your coins. Your storage media will suffer as well. If you have coins in holders of flips containing PVC, heat will speed up the PVC damage.

An important point is to not only dispose of plastic flips that contain PVC, but get rid of the plastic-vinyl album pages that contain the chemical. Fumes from PVC will seep into your neutral plastic holders stored in a PVC-laced vinyl page. As a general rule, most flips that contain PVC are soft and pliable, while most Mylar and other safe plastics are stiff and hard.

A closet shelf may come crashing down under the weight of the coins, and those under the bed will catch a lot of lint for the cat to play with. It's amazing how much a small box of coins will weigh.

Don't put them in a freezer, as crooks have learned that is the first place to look. A wall or floor safe, securely bolted down is one option, but you will probably have to compromise on a burglar proof safe, as the fire proof safes may contain chemicals that will damage your coins. Try and find a storage place that isn't that obvious, which also rules out the back of the closet. Think out of the box. For example, a box buried under old clothes in a clothes hamper is not likely to draw unwanted attention. Use your ingenuity.

Storage media is a hot topic. I'd suggest keeping an eye on your increasing number of coins. It's an

An important point is to not only dispose of plastic flips that contain PVC, but get rid of the plastic-vinyl album pages that contain the chemical.

excellent idea to start sorting and pick a value, perhaps $50 or $100. Any coin over the value you pick gets VIP treatment – storage in an inert, hard plastic holder. These are somewhat similar to the holders (slabs) used by the grading companies. They provide maximum protection, especially for proof or uncirculated coins.

"Always use products specifically designed for coins."

For a pot full of cents, or dozens of dimes, the next best things are inert plastic coin tubes. A glass prescription bottle may hold a handful of coins, but drop it and you'll be picking up glass splinters for days. The hard plastic holders give the coins the best possible protection. Make sure your budget includes proper storage media. Oddly enough, an exception to the rule are plastic bags used to hold various foods for human consumption.

Next come the plastic 2x2 coin flips and the matching paper ones. Make sure that you get rid of the PVC plastic. Mylar Flips will replace them, but can damage coins if they are moved in and out frequently.

The plastic and paper flips should not be used for long term storage – more than six months. Under exceptional conditions they will protect your coins over a longer span, but the big problem is that they are not air tight.

The same is true of the cardboard 2x2 holders. They have a Mylar window so that you can see both sides of the coin. These can be stapled shut, again with the warning not to get the staples or the stapler too close to the coin. To keep the coin safe the 2x2 needs to be stapled on the three open sides. Again the reminder to use your pliers to flatten the staple legs so they don't damage an adjacent coin. Staples will rust, but there are stainless steel staples on the market.

Next come coin folders and coin boards. These have holes for each date

Q:

What is nickel silver?

A:

It's an alloy of copper, zinc
and nickel, also known
as "German" silver. There
is no silver in the alloy,
despite the name.

and mint, and in some cases the outstanding minting
varieties, such as overdates. These are what you
most likely will use to start your collection.

The folders have a paper backing, so you can
see only one side of the coin. They expose the
visible side to the atmosphere and any pollution,
contamination or fingerprints. My recommendation
is that you use them for circulated coins that will
not show problems. Your uncirculated coins need
special protection and proof coins should be left in
their packaging.

The album pages allow seeing both sides of the
coin, usually held in place by plastic strips. This
type of album should also be used for circulated
coins, as the plastic strips can scratch the coins as
they slide back and forth. There are also albums
designed to hold the coins in inert plastic holders,
such as those used by the grading companies.
These of course can be used for proof coins and
uncirculated grade coins.

The artwork on the cover of this book, as I
mentioned in the Foreword, matches the cover art
on the Warman's coin folders, another part of F+W
Media. These folders are the basis for many, if
not most collections, because they provide several
collecting aides. There is a hole for coins for each
date. Under the hole is the mintage figure, which
tells you the relative rarity.

On the fly leaf are facts about the coins,
including the weight, diameter and composition,
all designed to simplify beginning your collection.
You can order the folders directly from the website,

Warman's coin folders

www.shopnumismaster.com, or you can probably find them at your local coin dealer's shop. They are still new to the marketplace, but with a little perseverance you can equip your burgeoning collection.

Canvas mint bags are among the poorer storage media. They obviously are not immune to water or contamination. Plus, every time the bag is moved the coins rub and scratch each other.

At the very bottom of the list are paper wrappers and the plastic tubes used by the Mint to ship coins. The paper wrappers offer only a bare minimum of protection. They tear easily, offer no protection from water damage and are easily penetrated by contamination. The "shotgun rolls" have the two end coins exposed. The soft plastic tubes also offer limited protection, with open ends. As with the paper wrappers, they should not be used for upper grade coins.

The odds are that you may have stored some coins in aluminum foil. This

Q:

Nickel coins are supposed to be magnetic. Doesn't mixing nickel with other metals in an alloy destroy this magnetic property?

A:

Pure nickel is slightly magnetic, but as little as 20 percent of some other metal added to it will destroy this magnetic property.

is something you need to immediately change. Any moisture will result in the metal-to-metal contact corroding the coin. I learned this after digging up several rolls of Morgan dollars that had been wrapped in foil and buried in the damp dirt floor of a garage. Every coin had suffered damage that no collector would want.

If you are using a shoe box for coin storage, you are running the risk of contamination. Trade it in for a plastic bin with a tight fitting lid, which will keep out anything in the air.

Summing up, it's very important that you take special care of your coins. I was as guilty as anyone of letting coins fend for themselves in cups or bowls that offered no protection. Nothing will hurt as much as to discover that a coin with some value has lost much of it due to scratches or dings inflicted while they were lying loose. Doing your housekeeping will pay big dividends.

Keep paper (except 2x2 coin flips) such as tissue paper, envelopes and cardboard away from your coins. Paper contains sulfur, which will turn your coins black. Cotton lined flips are relatively safe, but as with the regular flips, they should not be used for long term storage. A reminder again, use products specifically tested and intended for use with coins.

Even with the best of care, your proof and uncirculated coins may discolor or tarnish. In many cases this is from exposure prior to being packaged. Don't be surprised if your prize coin that's safely housed in a protective holder suddenly shows a

> Back during World War II they used a slogan to warn against giving information to the enemy: "Loose lips can sink a ship." Today you can lose your collection to a burglar by bragging about it, or openly displaying it.

fingerprint or a change in color. If you handled the coin correctly, the odds are that the coin was exposed before you got it.

Back during World War II they used a slogan to warn against giving information to the enemy: "Loose lips can sink a ship." Today you can lose your collection to a burglar by bragging about it, or openly displaying it. You need to impress on your relatives and friends that they are a risk to your collection if they talk about it to strangers, or even have their conversation overheard.

Coin dealers go to great lengths to overcome this problem. Gangs of thieves have been known to follow a dealer for miles when leaving a coin show and breaking into the vehicle when he stops for food or gas. As a collector you are not likely to face this problem unless you display a bunch of gold coins at the show. Use your head.

You can also rent a post office box so that your home address isn't on everything that comes to you through the mail. Address labels should be removed from all envelopes and other papers before they go in the trash or to be recycled. A paper shredder is a good investment.

CHAPTER 13

Got a
Question?

"There are no dumb questions."

We might give a dumb answer or two but as we said before, asking questions is the way to learn. Asking questions is not as easy as it sounds. Men are often accused of losing their direction but refusing to ask for help. Hopefully you don't fall in that category.

When you ask questions make sure you know where the answer is coming from. Unfortunately there are people who delight in giving wrong answers to questions that have been posted. They get their "fun" from the confusion they cause. If you have the slightest doubt, get a second opinion.

"Don't beat about the bush."

Frequently I get letters stating: "I have a coin. What is it worth?"

I certainly can't tell anything about that coin from the owner's all too brief description. Tell us as much about the coin as possible – denomination, date, mintmark, anything that looks "wrong." Always helpful is the apparent metal, especially for medals. A sketch and all the wording on both sides may be vital to identification, even if you include a photo or scan.

This is especially important if you are asking about a minting variety.

Photos or scans are useless if they are blurred, so get things in focus. Don't waste money on a professional photo until you have a firm value for your coin. Few professionals are equipped to photograph coins.

The alternative is a rubbing, either with a soft pencil or aluminum foil. The problem is that neither one will survive a trip through the mail. A pencil rubbing will smear and a foil rubbing will look like it had been run over by a road roller. You need to encase the rubbing in a reversed 2x2 cardboard holder or a small box, so that there is no pressure on the rubbing.

Don't be afraid to ask if you feel you have a coin that has potential value. All too many collectors decide their coin is rare and valuable so they sit on it, in hopes of finding more. I can count the fingers on one hand where a collector has found others, regardless of whether he had the first one appraised. If you discover a coin and report it for example to *Numismatic News*, your name is permanently associated with the find. If you "let George do it," George will get the credit for the find.

Often collectors are afraid, with good reason, that reporting their find might affect their personal security. I do as much as possible to avoid problems by only publishing first names. As most of you are aware, a full name and the home address can be found in seconds on the Internet. The last time I checked there were 16 Alan Herberts listed, including a Sir Alan in New Zealand and one in England. They have the wrong address for me, so I'm safe for the moment.

If incoming publications are a problem, you can in some cases get them sent to you in brown paper wrappers so that the neighbors don't see that you are a collector. Personal security is very important, so you need to do everything you can to protect it.

If you are writing to a publication, make sure your letter is addressed to the specific person or department, or publication. There are more than 30 publications under one roof at F+W Media, so the correct full address, including the name of the publication is very important.

Put your full name and address on both the letter and the envelope. Don't abbreviate the city and use the correct two-letter, all caps, no periods state

Q:

Supposedly there are eight "noble" metals, but my buddies are arguing about some of the less well known. Could you please list them?

A:

Besides gold, platinum and silver, the other five are members of the platinum group – palladium, rhodium, ruthenium, iridium and osmium. The noble metals are another way of designating those metals that are considered to be bullion, such as gold, silver and more recently platinum. The noble metals are contrasted with the base metals, such as lead, copper, tin, zinc or iron.

abbreviation. More than half of the mail has the wrong abbreviation or other error in the address, which often slows delivery. Do not use postcards. They are an open invitation to thieves. The few cents you save could cost you your collection.

Read the instructions as many times as it takes to learn them. Always remember return postage. Never use a small envelope or a card envelope when writing for information.

When you send a loose stamp don't staple or tape it to your letter. It will survive very nicely without being tied down. A stamp with staple holes is considered to have already been used and the post office may demand a new stamp.

If you are sending two or three things at once, address each separately and mark clearly where they are supposed to go. Even better, put them in separate addressed envelopes inside the main envelope.

Never send anything to F+W Media without a prior request. Don't send things to others through the mail without approval, as the post office considers unsolicited material as a gift, which does not have to be returned or paid for.

If you receive packaging instructions, follow them closely. Do not put tape on a coin. Tape the holder securely to a piece of cardboard and make sure the staples are flattened. As an example of poor packaging, put a loose nickel in a paper envelope. Hold the envelope by the end and snap it. The coin will fly across the room at bullet speed.

CHAPTER 14

PROOF COINS, PROOF AND MINT
SETS

I've mentioned proof coins several times, so I should explain them in more detail. Proof coins are made primarily for collectors. In the early history of our Mint, a proof coin was defined as a coin struck to test – or proof – the dies. Today, large numbers are struck for sale to collectors.

The first U.S. proof sets were offered for sale in the 1840s, although individual proofs appeared much earlier. Numismatic author Walter Breen quotes an 1858 notice by J. R. Snowden, offering sets for sale, but George F. Jones, in the *Coin Collectors Manual of 1860*, says that cased sets were sold as early as the 1840s. A set of minor coins with a face value of $1.94 sold for $2.02.

A Proof Set

Proof is not a grade, it is a condition. Worn or damaged proof coins are classed as impaired proofs. A proof coin is defined as one struck at least twice on a polished planchet by polished dies.

All three must apply or the coin is classed as a partial proof. American proof coins have mirror surfaces and a limited number have frosted devices. The central design is frosted, making a sharp contrast to the mirror fields.

Q:

Any hope of finding a small date 1982 cent on a brass planchet?

A:

There is a remote chance that a small date Denver cent on brass exists, if one of the old planchets was accidentally mixed in with the copper-plated zinc, but the only way you can tell for certain is to weigh the coin, as the zinc coins are 20 percent lighter than the brass.

Such proofs have their own grading system, as well as adjectival criteria such as "deep mirror" or "cameo" proofs. Proof coins in the same denominations as the circulating coins are usually housed in special hard plastic cases.

Single proof coins are usually issued in inert plastic capsules, which protect the surface and protect from damage. There also are reverse proofs, which have the reverse struck as a proof and a circulation die striking the obverse. Some early U.S. coins were struck with a proof obverse, since the coins would be displayed in a cabinet or other means which would hide the reverse.

Proof coin production was shifted to San Francisco in 1968, but in more recent times other

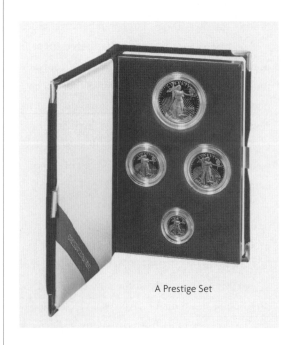

A Prestige Set

> *Common misconceptions about proofs include the tendency to call proof a grade when it is actually a condition of manufacture.*

mints have also struck proofs especially of commemorative or bullion coins.

Collectors are often surprised to find proof coins in circulation. Proofs are in fact legal tender and may be used like any other coin. There are two primary sources for such finds. Children may get into daddy's coin collection to buy ice cream or candy. Stolen coins are often spent, but the major source are dealers who open proof sets to remove an upper grade coin and dump the rest into their cash register, or their pocket.

The Mint packages various sets of coins. Proof sets contain proof versions of all of the circulating denominations from all of the mints. Certain sets, such as the Prestige sets, may contain one or more of the commemorative dollars for that year. All of the coins are proofs, in almost all cases in the same metal or alloy as the circulating coins. The Mint also strikes sets with 90 percent silver coins, beginning in 1992.

"Once a proof, always a proof."

Any proof showing wear is classed as an impaired proof. For more detail, read the *ANA Grading Guide* excerpts at the end of the book.

One of the fads of the 1960s is showing up again. The hook is "unopened mint packaging" with a small premium over opened packaging. There are two problems with this. One, you have no idea whether there really is a proof or mint set in that box, which could have been steamed open to remove the set and replace it with washers.

Two, you may be missing out on a valuable minting variety, such as the missing mintmarks on several proof coins. I repeat an old Yankee proverb at every opportunity: "Don't buy a pig in a poke."

A poke is defined as a sack. Sight unseen in this case is bad business.

Don't be surprised if you find more proofs than circulation strikes for

Q:

What do "Lg" and "Sm" refer to in ads for the 1982 cents?

A:

The Lg and Sm refer to the Large and Small date varieties for the different mints and different metals. The "Large" date is the same size as the 1981 date, while the "Small" is the same size as the 1983 date, with beveled edges on the letters and digits on the obverse.

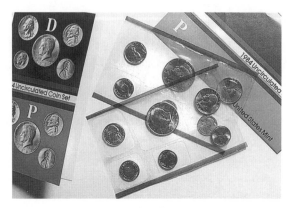

A Mint Packaged Mint Set

a given date—and prices to match. Collectors, if given a choice, tend to want proofs, leaving larger quantities in their hands with consequently lower prices.

You can easily fill a shelf in your library with books about proof coins. Be sure to have at least one book that fully explains the minting process by which all coins are made. When buying make sure you get a Mint-packaged set and not a substitute.

There are a few U.S. coins struck as matte proofs, but they are in the minority. Matte proofs are difficult to separate from regular coins because the principal differences are the sharp edges on the design elements.

Matte proofs have the same sharp edges on the design elements, but the surface is rough, in some cases even produced by sand blasting. The relatively few U.S. matte proofs are difficult to separate from the similar circulation strikes, except for the sharp-edged design elements.

Common misconceptions about proofs include the tendency to call proof a grade when it is actually a condition of manufacture. Don't feel bad if you have been misusing it, as a majority of collectors also mistakenly use condition when they mean grade for both proof and circulating coins.

Mint sets consist of examples of all the coins struck at all of the mints in a given year. Privately assembled mint sets may contain the same coins as a Mint-packaged set, but usually the Mint-packaged sets will sell at a premium. The coins in a Mint-packaged set have had at least some special care, but are usually difficult to distinguish from ordinary circulation strikes.

The Mint skipped making any Mint-packaged Mint sets in 1982 and 1983 as an economy measure. They resumed the sets in 1984 due to heavy pressure from collectors. Many privately packaged sets were made for those two years or a combination of Souvenir sets from the two mints were sold by dealers to fill the gap.

The Souvenir sets contain all the coins from a given mint for a given year and were sold only over the counter at the mints where the coins were struck. They are not recognized or listed in coin price guides because the Mint failed to keep any records of the numbers sold. When buying a Mint set, make sure it is a Mint-packaged set and not a substitute, and it should be priced accordingly.

A Privately Packaged Mint Set

CHAPTER 15

MINTMARKS

The odds are that at least one of the coins in your pocket will have a small letter near the date, or at some other place on the coin. That letter is a mintmark, placed to indicate the mint that struck the coin. The date of course is the year it was struck. The further odds are that if you live in the eastern part of the country that the letter will be a "P," and if you live in the middle or western part of the country the letter will be a "D," since that is the way the Mint's distribution is set up.

The P is the mintmark for the Philadelphia mint, while the D stands for the Denver mint. Philadelphia puts its "P" on all coins except the cent. When you look at proof coins, you will find an "S" for the San Francisco mint. There are two other current mintmarks, the "W" for West Point, N.Y., on a small group of coins, and the Denver "D."

The Carson City Mint

Historically, there are four other mints whose mintmarks appeared on our coins. The are:

"O" for New Orleans, La.

"CC" for Carson City, Nev.

"C" for Charlotte, N.C.

"D" for Dahlonega, Ga.

Note that there are two different mints using a "D," as the two mints did not operate at the same time.

The Philadelphia Mint

The U.S. has always used letters to identify the mints. Other countries have used letters, numbers or symbols to identify their mints.

Mintmarks are very useful to the collector, as they flag the mintages for a specific year and mint, pointing out the low mintage coins, which usually have more value than coins with higher mintages. The U.S. Mint experimented with removing mintmarks beginning in 1965, but bowing to collector pressure they restored them on the 1968 circulating coins.

The Denver Mint

Traditionally San Francisco coins have brought higher premiums due to lower mintages, but this comparison is no longer true in every case. For years collectors automatically saved anything with an "S" mintmark. From its establishment, San Francisco struck circulating coins, switching in 1968 to a mix of circulating and proof coins and later to nearly exclusive production of proof sets and commemorative coins. The history of the various mints is fascinating and worth a read at any time.

The San Francisco Mint

Q:
I thought when they restored the mintmarks to U.S. coins back in 1968 that it was mandatory?

A:
The law rescinding the five-year ban on mintmarks beginning in 1965 gave the Mint the "discretion" of restoring the mintmarks, rather than making it mandatory. That's a loophole any bureaucrat could drive a tank through.

CHAPTER 16

Minting
VARIETIES

Coins and stamps have several things in common, outstanding among them the high values attached to mis-strikes, or "errors," as they are universally incorrectly labeled. As you've seen, I've titled this chapter as "minting varieties" rather than "errors."

A Double
Struck Coin

The reason is very simple. Mint errors are only a part of a much larger group, which includes intentional changes, wear and tear on equipment and the third part, mint errors. I selected "Minting Varieties" as a name that would encompass all three divisions. It simply doesn't make sense to take a deliberate change in a die and call it an "error."

Intentional classes include many of the overdates, with one date punched over another to extend die life, or intentional changes in the design. Wear and tear applies to the wear on the minting equipment. Worn dies may exhibit die cracks or die breaks. Errors include actual mistakes that cover a wide variety of mishaps, such as double strikes or blundered dates.

Collecting minting varieties has often been described as the fastest growing part of coin collecting. While there is anecdotal evidence pointing in that direction there are conflicting claims. For example, the U.S. Mint estimates that 145 million people are collecting the State

A 1943/1942-P
Overdate Nickel

quarters. This figure is far higher than any previous estimate of collector numbers from any source.

I've mentioned the three principal divisions – planchets, dies and striking. Each of the three has numerous sections and classes. As I told the publisher, it would take a book to explain every one of the more that 400 classes. As it happens, there is such a book, the Seventh edition of *The Official Price Guide to Mint Errors and Varieties*. I wrote it and it is published by Random House, available in most large book stores.

Perhaps more than other areas of coin collecting, minting varieties require either extensive knowledge and experience or access to a specialist. An increasing number of coin dealers are specializing in varieties, but there still are numerous dealers who have no experience with them. Just as you wouldn't take a GM car to a Chrysler dealer for service, you need to find one of the specialists.

One of the more humorous things to come out of the early days of this specialty was the tendency to quote some local coin collector as the source saying, "I've never seen a coin like this, so it must be worth $50,000." I have never found anything explaining why $50,000 was such a popular price. This was at a time when four-figure prices for minting varieties were almost unheard of.

There are definitions for 416 classes of minting varieties in my book, covering everything from overdates to wrong planchets. This chapter is only a brief outline of the information that you will need to start collecting them. It's extremely rare for a cataloging system to be universally accepted, so I was fortunate to be able to produce an improvement over the "Major and Minor" classic partitions. Since the division system seems to work well, I'll use it to briefly touch on some of the highlights.

Planchets

First are planchets, the object that is struck by the die pair to produce a coin. The blanks are processed – punched from a strip of coin metal They become planchets by rolling them through an upsetting mill. This upsets the

Q:
An old book on the U.S. Mint mentions the job of "whitener." What did a whitener do?

A:
The whitener was the wash "lady" of the old mint and actually the job still is performed in today's minting operations. The whitener washed the planchets in a solution of borax, soap and water to remove the grease and dirt from the planchets, brightening them up for striking.

An Unstruck Planchet

edge, so there will be metal to form the design rim when they reach the coining press. At each step there is a variety of mishaps that can occur. The strip may slip, causing overlapping holes and clips, resulting in a missing part of the blank.

It takes a practiced eye to spot the difference between a legitimate minting variety and something produced by a shade tree mechanic. That's one reason why I stress looking at a lot of coins so that your eyes see any discrepancy. Clips can easily be faked, but there are certain telltale signs that cry "Fake!"

To name just a few of the planchet varieties, you may have blanks from the wrong coin metal strip (wrong stock) or you may have the right metal punched to the wrong size (wrong planchet). You may find planchets that were damaged before being struck. These too are hard to tell apart, but again there are usually clues to tell you which is which.

Blanks may bypass the upsetting mill and get struck by the dies. More clues. As you can already see, there is a lot to learn.

Planchets, or coins, can lose one or both

A Coin With a Clip

A Pair of Coin Dies

clad layers, separating from the core. Several metals or alloys are used for clad coins. Planchets may come from strip that was rolled too thin, or not thin enough. Thin layers of coin metal may separate from the planchet or coin.

Dies

It takes two to tango and it takes two dies to strike a coin. A very common misconception is that only one side of a coin is struck at a time, but that would be a violation of the "equal and opposite" forces of physics. The quickest way to demonstrate this is to hold a coin up in the air and hit at it with a hammer. Don't do this near a window.

One very significant characteristic are die varieties that repeat exactly on every coin struck by that die. If there is a die break on one coin you find, you can expect to find other coins with the same shape and size die break.

A 1955 Hub Doubled Cent

The die division is responsible for a majority of the

Q:

What's the difference between a brass cent and a brass-plated cent?

A:

A brass cent is entirely brass. A brass-plated cent has brass plating on some other metal or alloy.

classes, because there are so many different things that can happen to one or both dies. Of most interest to the public are any causes that result in doubling. F+W Media veteran numismatics editor David Harper is flooded with mail from people who have found what they believe is valuable doubling on a coin. He spends considerable time on such questions and I usually get any overflow.

The key problem is that there are at least 28 different forms of mint process doubling, plus some look-alike damage, making it doubly impossible to evaluate such coins without seeing them. Most of the forms have little or no collector value, something that is hard to explain to anyone who considers the slightest doubling on their coin as money in the bank.

There are two principal events that draw the most interest. The valuable one is hub doubling. The worthless one is machine doubling damage (MDD). The unfortunate part is that in certain forms the two are almost identical. The next most unfortunate part is that there are millions of MDD coins for every one with hub doubling. As a result, in all cases it takes authentication to prove which is which. Do not send the coin to F+W Media for authentication as we DO NOT do authentication work. Instead, consult the experts at CONECA – www.conecaonline.org. They charge an exam fee.

I'll repeat again: "You cannot fully authenticate a coin from a photo, as someone has to see the coin itself to determine the cause of doubling

> *The hard and fast rule here is never assume that the doubling on your coin has any value over face until it has been authenticated.*

and any value." Even the experts have been known to disagree over some unusual form of doubling. The hard and fast rule here is never assume that the doubling on your coin has any value over face until it has been authenticated.

Remember: You have at least 28 chances to be wrong.

Hub doubling is also known as a doubled die. Note the correct spelling, as it is frequently misspelled as a double die. It's safer to use hub doubling as there is less chance for misunderstanding. Double die is used as a name for worthless machine doubling damage and abrasion doubling, so it's important not to confuse the two spellings.

Besides doubling there are numerous classes in the die division. There are small dates, large dates, doubled dates, overdates, blundered dates and lettering, die breaks and die cracks – and many more.

Knowing what each one looks like is a major step forward if you decide to get into minting varieties. I started my collecting career with a 1935 cent that had glue on it. Under the glue it looked like a piece of gold struck into the coin. It would not be surprising if some event like that triggered a lifetime of collecting for you.

Striking

Here's where the rubber hits the road. This is where the planchet meets the die pair and becomes a coin. The blank has been changed into a planchet and is now being fed into the coin press that will change it into a coin.

A seemingly endless number of mishaps can occur until the struck coin drops down the coin press chute into a waiting receptacle. Coins get double struck, struck on top of other coins or planchets, or on oddball objects such

Q:

Is the master die ever used to strike coins?

A:

Under normal circumstances it would not be used since the master die is intended as a model from which to make the working hubs and then the working dies. However, the master die often was used to make trial strikes to demonstrate what the proposed coin would look like. In world coinage there are instances where the master die has been used in an emergency for coinage. The same thing has probably happened with U.S. coinage, but there is virtually no documentation of any such usage.

as washers, springs or screws. Coins may be struck on planchets with problems. Wrong size planchets may get into the feed, or the coin might be struck on a planchet for a foreign coin.

These and the dozens of classes I didn't mention, all have an irresistible pull for the curious collector. New classes turn up, keeping the excitement level high. At just about every major coin show in the last three or four decades some new and unexplainable coin showed up keeping us scratching our heads.

Because there are smaller numbers of collectors, it is more likely to find a minting variety with some value in your pocket. It is also possible to find a coin with two or three or more different minting varieties.

Don't trust your eyes to catch every variety, but 10X magnification is the maximum—if you can't see it with that it's of no value to collectors. Follow a routine on every coin you examine. That way you won't be kicking yourself for missing something important. Don't spend money on photographs until you are sure that your coin has value enough to cover the cost.

This advice is probably 180 degrees off of the position of the average collector. I get mail every day from people who are so convinced their coin is rare that they flatly refuse to let it out of their sight, or send it through the mail to get it authenticated. With a handful of exceptions, there isn't a city where you can get a coin authenticated. If you try to walk in with a coin you will be sent away – for

Damaged coins

THEIR protection – not yours. Mail, or a coin show are the only two ways to get a coin checked. Even at a coin show you may only get an opinion, not an authentication.

It's admittedly a steep learning curve for minting variety collectors, so be prepared to spend time learning the appearance and characteristics of the mis-strikes and oddities that come out of a mint. You especially need to learn the difference between coins that have been damaged, whether before, or after they were struck. The advantage to learning is that you will depend less and less on others to identify and evaluate your coins. Learning the minting process is a must, because once you know what should happen, it's easier to separate out the ones that had something else happen to them.

Another common mistake is to send "error" coins to the U.S. Mint, or the Federal Reserve Bank, expecting them to authenticate and place a value on

Q:

Some old books say that the 1944-1946 cents were "shell casing brass," made from salvaged shell casings, with a composition of 70 percent copper and 30 percent zinc. Modern catalogs call them "shell casing brass" but give the composition as 95 percent copper and 5 percent zinc. Which is correct?

A:

According to Ed Rochette, the original plan was to use the 70-30 alloy of the shell casings, but at the last moment enough copper became available to stay at 95-5.

the coin. The Mint does not authenticate, buy back its coins or even acknowledge them. The Mint is a manufacturing plant, not a coin dealer. The Fed is primarily a distribution center. You wouldn't send your antique car back to a plant in Michigan, so it's the same thing with coins.

Both David and I get frequent phone calls from collectors expecting us to place a value on their coins, especially those with doubling. For the umteenth time, you cannot accurately evaluate a coin without seeing it, so contact an authenticator at CONECA.

In this chapter you have seen a lot of new terms that need further explanation, or a description. You will find some of the definitions in the glossary at the end of this book, but for some others you will need my other book. One of the unexpected benefits when writing definitions for each class was that any time there was an apparent need for a footnote, it was actually a signal that a new or different class had to be added, so there are no footnotes in any of the classes.

The advice about not buying coins sight unseen applies doubly to minting varieties offered on the Internet. Most of the varieties offered are mislabeled, due to a lack of knowledge on the part of the seller. If you are lacking in experience it's a double whammy. Besides incorrect labels, it's a good bet that any photo shown may not be that of the offered coin. There is a lot of "borrowing" going on. While there are legitimate dealers offering coins there is a tendency with other offers

A row of coin presses.

to evoke the "Dumb selling to the dumber" characterization. Repeating the Yankee expression I append to this:

"Don't buy a pig in a poke."

Most collector coins start at face value and increase slowly, often over a period of years or decades. The marked difference with minting varieties is that they have "instant" value. This means that the moment you find one, you can offer it for sale and expect to get more than face value for it.

One of the key rules affecting minting varieties is that "helped" coins are unacceptable. Over the years there have been a number of instances of mint employees deliberately creating minting varieties, which are classed as Mint

Q:

Why is it that if you add up the individual prices of the coins in a proof set it is much higher than the cost of the set?

A:

In the world of commerce the sum of the parts is a multiple of the whole. If you went out and bought all the parts to make a car to assemble yourself, the parts would cost several times more than buying a complete car, and the same is true of coins.

Sports. One that sticks in my mind were a number of nails struck by coin dies. There was also a rash of folded coins, some of which wouldn't have fit in the coining chamber of a coin press.

Another classic helped coin was a 1930 New Mexico tax token, overstruck with 1970 proof dime dies. The rule here is that anything larger than the feed tube would have to have been helped. This means that you can't have a cent overstruck by dime dies without being helped. The same rule applies to proof coins. If it won't fit in the plastic holder, then it has been helped out of the mint. This is the rule the Secret Service follows.Many paper money collectors are avid error collectors, but that's a whole different ball game. Coins are minted, paper money is printed, so collecting paper errors requires detailed knowledge of the printing process. There are several excellent books on the printing process.

The learning curve for minting variety collectors is quite steep and often hampered by the numerous slang terms and nicknames that are in common usage. If you do have an all-consuming thirst for the unexpected, this is certainly an area to explore.

Collecting minting varieties requires a thorough knowledge of the minting process and what it can and can't do to a coin. It requires the ability to recognize mint-process results from accidental or deliberate damage.

Yes, people do deliberately mutilate coins, either for spite, or to sell to some novice as a "real error." Even Mint employees have been known to deliberately create "errors" for sport, waiting to see how many collectors fall for it. An altered coin is usually not collectible. However, it's good to know that some artistic alterations, such as the "Hobo" nickels or love tokens are highly collectible. Ironically, those Hobo nickels have been heavily copied in recent years.

As with any special coin, prices for state quarter minting varieties have gone through the roof. As one example, all five of the 1999 State quarters from both the Philadelphia and Denver mints were found with rotated reverses, some as much as 180 degrees, or half a circle. Prices for the larger rotations peaked for a short time in the $500 range. There are three die varieties of the Wisconsin quarter. Sets of the three sold for as much as $1,100. Off-center strikes, double strikes and other significant minting varieties are bringing large multiples of the same variety on an ordinary Washington quarter.

I'll be glad to answer your questions; you may contact me via e-mail at AnswerMan2@aol.com.

Q: I have a set – a pair of gold plated Bicentennial half dollars with a special gold stamp. Can you tell me what this set is worth?

A:
The set that you have has two coins worth a face value of one dollar and an undetermined amount of gold in the stamp. The plating on the coins contains only a few cents worth of gold, and destroys any numismatic or collector value the pieces might have had.

CHAPTER 17

COMMEMORATIVE COINS

In general, commemorative coins are made for collectors. However, there are exceptions, most notably the recent State quarters, the Lewis and Clark nickels and the 2009-2010 Lincoln cents. They and the Ike dollars are circulating commemoratives. A commemorative coin obviously recognizes, or commemorates something. The circulating Bicentennial quarters, halves and dollars, marking the 200th anniversary of our nation.

Regular commemoratives fall roughly into two groups – those struck between 1892 and 1954 – and the second group, struck since 1976. Some are struck as proofs, but in some instances, such as the special uncirculated Ike dollars, they didn't have a proof finish. Each of the commemoratives required an Act of Congress (a law), so they were ultimately able to control the issues.

One of the unexpected boundaries of the commemorative issues not intended for circulation is that collectors only want examples in the very highest grades. There is almost no aftermarket for lower grade pieces, which typically had been carried as a pocket piece. In many cases the bullion value exceeds the collector value of any lower grade piece. Coin price guides usually only list the about uncirculated and uncirculated or proof grades.

The appearance of circulating commemoratives, such as the Washington quarter, the Eisenhower dollar and the State quarters has changed the

A commemorative coin

An 1892
Columbian
Exhibition
Commemorative

commemorative market, because now it is possible to find a commemorative in your pocket change. This used to be the way almost all coins were collected. The U.S. Mint and other world mints have discovered that making commemoratives is a good way to plump up the bottom line.

Since 1982 the commemoratives have expanded significantly. Where the earlier commemorative series were almost all limited to half dollars, the Mint began production of commemorative dollars in 1983 with the Olympic dollars, the $5 Half Eagles in 1986, the $10 Eagles in 1984 and the $20 Double Eagles in 2009. A variety of sets have been produced, usually concentrated on a single theme.

There are several excellent books on commemorative coins that you will want for your library. Repeating a word of warning, beware of so-called commemorative "coins" that are actually medals struck by private mints.

The definition of a coin is simple—a piece issued by a government body and assigned a specific value for commerce. If the piece in question doesn't match the definition, then it's not a coin.

Q:
Are there any U.S. coins with ads on them?

A:
While not strictly ads, several U.S. coins identify commercial companies. The 1925 Ft. Vancouver commemorative half has the words "Founded by Hudson Bay Company." Also, there's the Pass & Stowe firm name on the Liberty Bell, which is found on the Ike dollars, the 1926 Sesquicentennial half dollars and the Franklin halves.

CHAPTER 18

Non-Circulating
Legal Tender

One term that you will run into as a collector is non-circulating legal tender or NCLT for short. The term applies to our proof and bullion coins because while they are not intended for circulation, they do have a stated value and can be used for business.

Outside the U.S. the term is applied to coins that are issued by a particular government, but banks in that country will refuse to accept them. This often occurs with commemorative issues that are treated the same as ours, up to the point where they are refused by the banks.

Actually, most collectors ignore the legal status of the coins, adding them to their collection without even considering whether they are or aren't legal tender.

This might be a good place to briefly discuss legal tender. As stated on our notes, and applying to our coins, they are legal "to pay all debts, public or private."

Many people misunderstand this phrase, believing that notes or coins MUST be accepted, but that is not what the law covers. The legal tender currency MAY be used, but there is nothing in the law requiring that it be accepted. This is a point that is often the topic of heated argument by the misinformed.

CHAPTER 19

WORLD
COINS

I've mentioned world coins several times, but they deserve a little better explanation. At one time there were thousands of mints. That number has narrowed down to about 70 worldwide. There were hundreds of private mints in the U.S. turning out art bars in the 1970s, but all but two or three have closed their doors as the art bar fad faded away.

The vast majority of U.S. collectors stick to U.S. coins. Any side trips are likely to Canada, Mexico or Great Britain. Language plays a key role, as many collectors are afraid to venture into other countries because of language problems.

The answer, not unexpectedly, is a catalog. The Krause Publications *Standard Catalog of*

An English coin

World Coins (now a division of F+W Media), was first issued in 1972. It had a revolutionary effect on the coin collecting hobby in Europe and I had a front row seat in 1975, spending two years in Germany promoting the catalog, going to coin shows and visiting mints. While there were ample catalogs in the native languages, this was the first compilation of coins from a number of different countries, all in English and with thousands of photos, far more than most other catalogs. The Krause catalogs revolutionized coin collecting around the world.

The catalogs drew many American collectors to collecting world coins.

Anxiety over minting methods and suspect mintage figures gave way to trusted information.

These are problems that are slowly fading away as more knowledge of the minting process is available. The majority of mints around the world use the same methods as the U.S. Mint – and often the same equipment – to produce their coins. With the exception of a handful of countries, most are willing to post accurate mintage figures in published price guides.

It may surprise you to learn that some countries will not issue mintage figures or other information about their coins. The Krause Catalog Department depends on a network of collectors and dealers to contribute and provide missing information. Many of these consultants are on the ground in the country they specialize in.

Today the *Standard Catalog* has been repeatedly expanded and revised. It has grown so big that it is now divided by century, each sporting a telephone book size catalog. Besides the Standard Catalog, F+W Media also produces the monthly *World Coin News* newspaper for world coin collectors and *Bank Note Reporter* which covers both U.S. and world paper money, plus the *Standard Catalog of® World Paper Money*, the *Standard Catalog of® United States Paper Money* and the *Standard Catalog of® Small Size U.S. Paper Money*. Some of these catalogs also come as CD sets. More recently catalogs for individual world states, countries or groups of countries are being produced.

U.S. collectors are not left out, with the

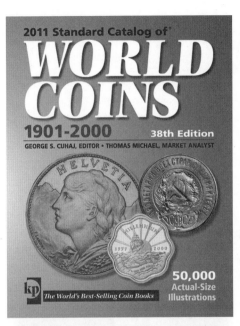

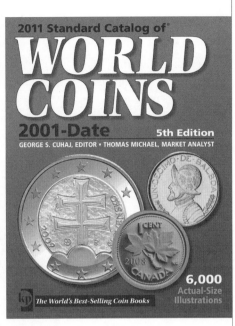

Today the Standard Catalog has been repeatedly expanded and revised. It has grown so big that it is now divided by century, each sporting a telephone book size catalog.

Q:

Did the slang term "buck" for a dollar have anything to do with the deer population in our forests?

A:

"Buck" is traced to the Ohio area and several others, where deer skins were at one time or another used as money, a prime hide being worth about a dollar. "Long Green" is another such term, coming from the tobacco money of Virginia and Maryland.

Numismatic News periodical covering collector activity all over the country. *Coins* magazine features stories and columns about popular U.S. collector coins. *Coin Prices*, another periodical, has all the latest values for every U.S. coin and comes out every two months. You can order subscriptions or a catalog by calling (800) 367-9723, or by going to www.krause.com.

Krause also publishes the monthly *World Coin News*, which carries the latest news about new issues and information about other aspects of collecting world coins. For paper money collectors, there is the *Standard Catalog of® World Paper Money* book and *Bank Note Reporter* monthly.

CHAPTER 20

GRADING
COINS

Reading through to here, you've seen repeated references to grading. This chapter will go into it in some depth, because of its importance to the collectors and dealers.

The current grading system is based on 70 numerical grades, ranging from the poorest at one to the ultimate at 70. The numerical system has essentially eclipsed the adjectival grading system in use for seven or eight decades. The principal reason for its adoption is that the numerical system is less subject to abuse. Terms used in adjectival grading were subject to interpretation, meaning that each dealer had his own definition for a given grade. "Brilliant Uncirculated" could cover several numerical grades, each differently defined.

"My coins are in very good condition." That is an almost universal description of coins that the general public asks about. The average person doesn't know that "very good" is near the bottom of the wear scale. The word "condition" ends the discussion, because a grade is not a condition. The founding fathers of our hobby could have saved all of us a lot of grief if they had used more apt terms.

"Why a 70-point scale?" Why indeed. It would have been much simpler to use a 100-point scale, or more practically, a 50-point scale, but Dr. William Herbert Sheldon's 70-point scale for grading large cents was hauled out of its bed and converted to general coin grading. "Fair" or "Poor" had been suggested adjectival grades for low end coins, but got dropped by

Q:

A coin I sent to a grading service was returned with the notation that it had been "whizzed." What does this mean?

A:

It means that your coin has been altered. The ANA definition is: "The artificial treatment of a coin by wire brushing, acid dipping or otherwise removing metal from the coins's surface to give it the artificial appearance of being in a higher grade."

the wayside. Much more attention was applied to the new Mint State (MS) grades from 60 to 70. The MS-60 to MS-65 grades cover most of the uncirculated coins, with much smaller numbers approaching the elusive MS-70, with only a handful of examples in that grade.

"Learn to do your own grading so that you never have to depend on someone else's grading skill."

A number of third party grading companies are available to get your coin graded and slabbed. They have made a thriving business by standardizing grading and separating out coins that have been doctored or cleaned.

The main reason the MS grades are very important is because in today's coin market a single point can mean a difference in value of hundreds or even thousands of dollars. It's well worth spending time on learning to grade for yourself.

The 59 different lower points are based on the exact amount of wear. The upper 11 are all uncirculated and don't show any wear, so their grades have slightly different criteria. Descriptions used in the grading guide may be difficult to understand, but there are photo charts showing coins in the different grades that are very helpful, and can be found at the end of this book. The American Numismatic Association has published the *Official Grading Standards for U.S. Coins*, which goes into grading in much more detail. A portion of the grading guide is included in the appendix.

Unfortunately, there is no single standard

> *The main reason the MS grades are very important is because in today's coin market a single point can mean a difference in value of hundreds or even thousands of dollars. It's well worth spending time on learning to grade for yourself.*

for grading. Besides the original scale, instituted by the ANA, each of the grading firms have their own interpretation of the definitions for each grade. Most are nearly the same, but expressed in slightly different language. The often-subtle differences may extend to slightly different standards for different series of coins.

My standard advice is to collect only those coins you need to complete a series and to fill the family albums. Collect them in the best grade possible, preferably the highest possible uncirculated grade. It should tell you something that almost 40 years later, we still list only face values for circulated Bicentennial quarters. Cash in 15 or 20 of the circulated coins and buy a MS-65 grade for your collection.

When you reach the point where you can consistently grade within a single point, then you are far better equipped to buy coins for your collection. Since most coins are priced by their grade, you can save a substantial amount by being able to determine the actual grade of the coin. By learning to grade, you gain the knowledge to spot over-graded coins and also the rare bargains that have been under-graded.

Looking back at adjectival grading, the many terms used to describe coins often conflicted, and even more, often confused the potential buyer. A few took advantage of the system and used the multitude of terms to deliberately mislead the buyer. In many instances, it is necessary to query the dealer for a definition of a term before buying to ensure you are getting the grade you want.

Numerical grading is intended to cure these language problems for everyone's benefit. Many of us didn't like numerical grading when it was introduced in the early 1980s, but after seeing it in use, I am now satisfied

Q:

I thought the Constitution prohibited anyone but the federal government from minting coins. How did private mints like those in California get away with violating the law?

A:

The prohibition in the Constitution is worded to prevent the States from coining money, but since nobody happened to think of private mints the point was overlooked in the original document, and remained legal until it was outlawed later.

that it is serving its purpose. Wait until you are comfortable with your grading ability before buying coins that you haven't had a chance to examine.

"Don't be paranoid about your coins and their value."

There are people who have convinced themselves that the grading service is going to switch coins, or that a local coin dealer is going to switch the coin in a matter of seconds while examining it. As I pointed out before, the dealer is probably more worried that the customer is trying to pull a fast one.

The final chapter in this book is a condensed version of the *Official ANA Grading Standards for U.S. Coins*. It will give you a better idea of the way numerical grading works.

CHAPTER 21

COINS AS AN
INVESTMENT

In my years in the hobby I have tried to stay away from offering coin investment advice and encouragement. When I do offer advice it can be summed up in a single word – Don't. You can lose your shirt just as quickly in coins as with any other commodity.

Before you turn the page, let me explain. Sowbellies, wheat, corn and a hundred other commodities are bought, sold or traded. It's a big business. A really big business. Coins are also a big business. My point here is, do you know the first thing about any of these products? Do you know the first thing about coins?

I'm so sure that you don't that I'll proceed with that assumption. You are not likely to jump in, checkbook at the ready, on those other commodities, so why do you think you will do any better with coins? If all you have to go on is a newspaper story that a single coin sold for over $3 million, then you are in for a very rude awakening.

When I get a message asking for investment advice, my usual response is: "Come back in 15 to 20 years when you have gained experience as a collector."

That's the kind of experience you urgently need before your checkbook comes into play.

There are coin experts and dealers who do offer investing advice, much like a stock broker, but you have to dig to find them. Many coin dealers offer investment advice, but their expertise often is at a lower level. At that, it is

A:
Clad coinage has been around for some time. The Greeks instituted a silver clad copper coinage after C.E. 700.

Gold bars

better than the daily pitches to buy gold coins from TV spokesmen who drop, scrape and rub their coins, rather than give them the delicate handling they require. It's easy to count the "experts" who ignore the "hold it by the edge" rule.

As you gain experience as a collector, these bits of advice will serve you well. We all want our collections to be much more valuable that the amount we have put into them. As your experience grows, so will the value of your collecting.

Now, a very important point. When you are tempted to invest in coins, the quoted price in a price guide is not what you will pay. The dealer is going to take a bite off of both ends of the deal. His profit margin may range from 20 to 50 percent and in some cases even more. This is by no means unique to the coin hobby.

Then, when you sell the coin, the dealer takes off another percentage. This means that you will have to wait – sometimes decades – for the coin to appreciate enough to offset the two bites so that you show some extra value. I told you this was not going to be easy.

If you are a beginning collector, even a moderately experienced collector, you are not ready to consider coins as an investment. Many greenhorns come with checkbook waving, expecting instant profits and a life of luxury. It does not work that way.

Would you go blindly into the stock market without researching the company whose stock you want to buy? Why then would you think that investing in coins doesn't need any preparation?

You can lose your shirt just as easily buying or selling coins as you can buying sow bellies or a thousand shares of Shady Deal stock.

You will find plenty of TV pitchmen selling you coins. You will find telemarketers selling you coins. They and others pitch coins as the best investment going. Reread the line above.

Don't go away mad. As you become a smart collector, you will find that many of the coins you already have are sporting a very nice premium. In the long term, coin prices as a group increase. Individual coins in that group can and do go down.

However, the questions roll in and the best answer I have is that my crystal ball is too cloudy and cracked to be of any help – and if it did help, I'd be using the knowledge to make myself rich. The hard facts is that there is no way to predict the coin market any more than you can predict how the stock market is going to do from day to day.

Some good pieces of advice repeated here. Collect what you like, not what someone tells you to collect, or the latest pitch on your TV.

Many greenhorns come with checkbook waving, expecting instant profits and a life of luxury. It does not work that way.

Q:

Are the 1982 zinc cents the same as the 1943 "lead" cents?

A:

There is a persistent misconception that the current cents should be magnetic. The 1943 cents were commonly called "lead" cents, but were actually zinc-plated steel. From mid-1982 the cents are now copper-plated zinc. The 1943 cents are magnetic because of the steel core, while the 1982 and later cents are not. Zinc has no magnetic properties.

"Beware of fire-sale prices."

The overwhelming odds are that there will not be a bargain. "Don't buy anything offered in a cold call from someone you don't know." Avail yourself of the benefits of having your phone number – and cell phone number – on the national "Do Not Call" list. However, don't forget that the rules exempt firms with which you have done business, so don't give them a head start.

Investing in gold, platinum or silver bullion is entirely another matter. Precious metals go by different rules than the coins made from them. Consider this: when you buy gold in the form of bars, you are entering a market that is dominated by the Central Banks of many of the major nations around the world. Your hundreds of dollars are matched against millions of dollars, even billions of dollars worth of gold. You are taking on bankers with decades of experience who can dump tons of gold on the market literally at a moment's notice. Remember, you are thinking in ounces, while they are thinking in tons.

Copper is not bullion, although the U.S. Mint sometimes handled it like bullion. Copper has generated many a fantasy as prices exceeded the melt value of our copper-alloy coins. Collectors thinking in ounces neglected that copper is sold by the pound. Tons of cents have been hoarded with the expectation of huge profits. The problem is they forgot to charge the smelting costs, labor and transportation.

Just as there are fake and altered coins, so too, are there fake bullion bars. It may be a gold bar with the center hollowed out and filled with lead. It may be a solid block of lead with gold plating. This means that before you sell your bars, you may have to pay for an expensive assay. With bullion coins, this is not usually a problem.

Platinum markets are equally as volatile and there is far less platinum than gold available. Currently platinum is selling for roughly twice the value of gold, but it wasn't that long ago that the two metals were neck and neck in price.

Silver brings with it a wholly different set of circumstances. It's much more plentiful than either gold or platinum. It was the key metal in the Hunt family's attempt to corner the metals market in 1980, when the price went to $52 an ounce.

As this is being written, silver is slightly above $17 an ounce. Thousands of investors are sitting on silver that they bought for $20 or more an ounce. Most of them will sell out if the price of silver ever gets back to what they paid. The deciding factor is India. Reliable reports indicate that there is enough silver buried in that country to meet demands for silver for several decades. If silver prices go up, that silver will be dug up again and will flatten the world market for the metal. Don't believe the hucksters who claim all the silver is used up.

Last call: if you do decide against all advice to invest in gold, be absolutely certain that you are getting delivery of what you pay for. One of the biggest scams is the company that offers to store your gold or gold coins while you are paying for them, and even after, then disappears when it's time to pay up.

Take possession of what you buy and store it in the safest possible place, with the keys in your possession. In the past, there have been dozens of companies pulling this scam, leaving investors with worthless receipts.

Remember the adage, "Don't put all your eggs in one basket."

CHAPTER 22

COLONIAL
COINS

With this chapter I'm going to begin to list specific coins that you can collect. Again I'm not recommending any particular coin to collect, just showing you what's out there. An important segment of our coinage are the Colonial coins, struck by several of the colonies before they were united. They have their own listings, separate from our Federal coinage.

A vital point – almost every Colonial coin has been copied and recopied. The overwhelming odds are that almost any Colonial piece you come in contact with (except from a dealer) is a worthless or near-worthless copy.

Thousands upon thousands of fake Continental dollars and New England shillings are among the common copies.

The key advice here is finding a catalog and then finding a dealer who specializes in Colonials. A dealer or a collector will be your only source for Colonial coins, so it's important to find someone who is willing to share their knowledge. If you are on the Internet, you can find a list of dealers by specialty at the American Numismatic Association website at www.money.org.

Q:
Did the early silver proof sets contain only silver coins?

A:
They also contained the "minor" coins, first the cent, later the 2-cent, then the copper-nickel 3-cent and nickel.

When considering a Colonial coin, check the edge. If there is a raised ridge of coin metal, or evidence it has been removed, then the piece is undoubtedly a worthless cast copy.

If Colonials catch your fancy and you can afford them, by all means, go ahead. However, starting with something this difficult to collect should give you pause while you learn more about collecting in general.

CHAPTER 23

HALF CENTS

Beginning with this chapter I'm going to briefly describe each Federal denomination and some of the highlights of that particular coin. The half cent is the smallest denomination struck by the U.S. Mint.

They were important to commerce, as in the early days there were a multitude of foreign coins in circulation with differing values, so that making change was often a real headache. The half cents were struck from 1793 to 1857, so you won't find one in circulation. Those with dates from 1840 to 1849 list at $1,000 in Good-4, the lowest acceptable grade.

There are five series designs for the half cents. The Liberty Cap was only struck in 1793. The Liberty Cap facing right was produced from 1794 to 1797. Next was the Draped Bust (1800-1808), the Classic Head (1809-1836) and the Braided Hair, struck from 1840 to the end of the denomination in 1857. Prices in Good-4 grade are all over the map, as high as $27,000 for the 1796 "No Pole" variety.

Q:

Both my 1975 and 1976 proof sets have the same Bicentennial quarters, halves and dollars. Is this a mistake?

A:

Both the 1975 and 1976 proof sets contained the Bicentennial quarters, halves and dollars, so both are normal sets for the year. There were no quarters, halves or dollars struck bearing a 1975 date. The Mint felt that there wouldn't be time to gear up for the extra production of the 1976-dated quarters, halves and Ike dollars.

CHAPTER 24

CENTS

You call them "pennies," but they are not pennies. They are cents. Right on the coin it says "ONE CENT." Penny is a throwback to our English heritage, as the English have used pennies for over a thousand years. In the U.S., it's a slang term that's impossible to eradicate. Even the Mint has thrown in the towel and refers to them as "pennies" in its literature. Actually, the change to "cent" was a deliberate attempt by the founding fathers to distinguish our coinage from the English "penny."

The cent is an important coin for collectors. Until recently, it was the most common coin to be found in a collector's hands. Most older collectors started with a cent coin board or folder when they were young, working up from that to other denominations.

The large cent wasn't called that until after 1857, when the series ended and the smaller diameter and lighter Flying Eagle cents were issued. The Large cent is unique in that three different designs were used in 1793, the first year of issue. The Flowing Hair cent with chain reverse was the first, followed by the Flowing Hair with wreath reverse and the Liberty Cap. A slightly different Liberty Cap was struck in 1795 and 1796. The Draped Bust cent finished 1796 and went on to 1807, followed

by the Classic Head design from 1808 to 1814.

No cents were struck in 1815, the only break in that denomination. The Coronet design lasted from 1816 to 1839, followed by the Braided Hair cent from 1840 to the last large cent in 1857.

The Flying Eagle cent began in 1856 with an estimated mintage of 2,500. Some 17.4 million were struck in 1857 and 24.6 million in 1858. The short series included an 1858/7 overdate and large- or small-motto 1858 varieties. All of the Flying Eagle cents were struck on copper-nickel planchets.

The Flying Eagles were replaced in 1859 by the Indian Head cent, also on copper-nickel planchets. In 1860, a shield was added at the top of the reverse. There were three varieties for 1864, the shield reverse on copper nickel, and the same design on bronze plus a design adding an "L" to the ribbon, identifying James Longacre as the designer.

The Indian Head was replaced in 1909 by the Lincoln cent and lots of controversy. Victor David Brenner (VDB) put his initials on the lower reverse of the 1909 cents, only to have it removed in mid-year and not restored until 1918 on the base of the bust on the obverse. This makes the 1909-S VDB cent one of the key coins in the Lincoln cent series.

Q:

What does an ad mean when it says "a mixed roll of Lincoln cents?"

A:

The usually accepted meaning is that it will be a roll with a number of different dates and mints in various grades. Left unsaid is whether there are or aren't a number of duplicates.

Design changes and minting varieties abound. The cent had a wheat-head wreath until 1958 and the Lincoln Memorial reverse since 1959. The modern Lincoln cent has a couple of outstanding hub-doubled coins, the 1955 and 1972, plus the large-and small-date 1960 cents.

The cent holds the record for alloy changes. The copper large cents, the copper-nickel Flying Eagles, the copper-nickel and bronze Indian Head cents, the bronze, brass and zinc-plated steel and the current copper-plated zinc on the Lincoln cent, make a total of six different metals or alloys. A common mistake at all levels is to refer to "copper" cents when the correct term (except for the large cents) is copper-alloy.

CHAPTER 25

2 CENTS

Some of you younger collectors may not even know that we once had a 2-cent coin, as well as a three-cent coin. The 2-cent was introduced in 1864 as the Civil War was starting to wind down.

It was struck until 1873, so it's also a very short series. Two varieties of note: the 1864 comes with large or small motto and also comes with various amounts of rotation of the reverse die. Turn the coin over top to bottom to catch the rotations.

CHAPTER 26

3 CENTS

The 3-cent coins came in two flavors – copper-nickel and silver. The silver came first, in three distinct varieties between 1851 and 1873. The Type 1 had no outline of the star. It was replaced in 1854 by the Type 2 with three outlines and again in 1859 with the Type 3 with two outlines

The first ones were only 75 percent silver, but fell into line as a 90 percent silver coin in 1854.

The copper-nickel three-cent coin production overlapped part of the silver, beginning in 1865 and ending in 1889. Both kinds were cordially disliked by the public because of their small size – both are smaller than a dime – which made them easy to lose. However, their popularity with collectors is readily apparent when you read their price chart.

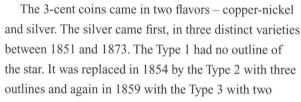

A Copper-Nickel
3-Cent Piece

Silver 3 Cents Type II

Silver 3 Cents Type III

CHAPTER 27

HALF DIMES

Our 5-cent coin has been called a nickel ever since 1866, when it was first introduced. The earliest form of a 5-cent coin were the silver half dimes. The half-dimes were among the first coins struck by the U.S. Mint in 1793 and maintained an odd 89.2 percent silver content until mid-1837, when another 0.8 percent silver brought them up to full strength. The half-dime minting varieties would keep any collector hopping.

Like the larger-denomination silver coins, it went through the Flowing Hair, Draped Bust with small eagle, Draped Bust with heraldic eagle and Liberty Cap. Then came the Seated Liberty with no stars, with stars, drapery added to left elbow, arrows at date, arrows removed and the final issues from 1860 to 1873 with "UNITED STATES OF AMERICA" replacing the stars.

Q:

I'm told that at one time the half dime and dime were depicted on mail as postage. Is there any truth to the story?

A:

Both designs in the form of hand stamps were in fact used to show postage had been paid, and in addition the 3-cent silver coins were in a few rare cases glued to the envelope as prepayment, and at least one post office used a hand stamp with the 3-cent design including the word "PAID." Prepayment of postage became universal in the U.S. in 1855.

CHAPTER 28

5-CENT NICKELS

The 5-cent nickel, actually copper-nickel, was a pleasant surprise for mint officials, as it was gladly accepted by the public, in marked contrast to the usual scorn greeting new designs. The chief grumble was the incorrect presumption that the 1866 design intentionally glorified the Stars and Bars of the Confederacy. Following the Shield design of 1866-1882 were the Liberty nickels of 1883-1913. That series had the distinction of a major variety at beginning and end – the 1883 "No Cents" and the five clandestine 1913 nickels now worth more than a million dollars each.

Then came the Indian Head nickel, quickly renamed by the public for the big Buffalo on the reverse, avoiding confusion with the Indian Head cents still very much in circulation. Two major varieties in this series are the 1918/1917-D overdate and the 1937-D three-legged Buffalo.

The design was changed in 1913, removing the mound the Buffalo stands on.

Q:
I saw an ad offering an 1883 gold coin, described as a "racketeer nickel." What's it supposed to be?

A:
The coin offered is an 1883 nickel that has been gold plated to simulate a $5 gold piece. These were passed on unsuspecting people when they were first issued because the nickel didn't have the denomination spelled out. For this reason they became known as "racketeer nickels," but there is no guarantee that the coin you buy today was plated in 1883. It is not a gold coin, just a gold-plated nickel.

Q:

Is it true that two war nickels contain more silver than a 90 percent silver dime?

A:

A fact being constantly overlooked: a 90 percent silver dime contains .0724 ounce of silver, while a single wartime nickel contains .0563 ounce. Thus, two nickels contain .1126 ounce of silver. For that matter, three nickels contain .1689 ounce and a silver quarter contains just .1809 ounce. If the Mint had gone ahead with the original plans for a 50 percent silver nickel in 1942, it would have resulted in a coin which would contain .0804 troy ounce of silver!

The Jefferson nickel is still with us, starting in late 1938 after the last of the Buffalo nickels were struck. Included in this series are the war-time nickels with a low-grade silver alloy replacing precious copper and a very large mintmark over the dome on the reverse. Years later, a 1943/1942 overdate was discovered.

Popular with collectors are fully struck coins with complete steps on the reverse. Some dates

Q:

I have a thin coin that is smaller than normal. The diameter is less, and the design seems to be reduced to match.

A:

Smaller and thinner means the coin has been reduced with acid. These pieces usually are thinner than a normal cent and have a generally "fuzzy" surface appearance. The key point in identification is that the design is essentially complete even on a paper thin coin. This would not happen with a genuine thin planchet strike.

with five or six full steps are rare to extremely rare.

Riding on the popularity of the State quarters, a group of four new nickel designs were released, beginning in 2004, honoring the Lewis and Clark expedition. The Buffalo reappeared on the reverse of the 2005 nickels, turned 180 degrees to face right rather than left. Jefferson has a new look as well. The 2006-2007 coins show a facing portrait of Jefferson, with an enhanced Monticello reverse.

CHAPTER 29

10-CENT
DIMES

They didn't get around to striking the first dimes until 1796, but a slow start has been followed by tremendous production figures. Not exactly a popular coin, it still figures prominently in commerce. It, too, didn't reach 90 percent silver until 1837, going through several designers. There were two periods of arrows added to the date 1853-1855 and 1873-1874, the first for a slight decrease, the latter indicating a slight increase in weight. The series was replaced by the Barber dime in 1892, the Mercury dime in 1916 and the Roosevelt dime in 1946. The latter, like the designs for the quarter, changed from silver to copper-nickel clad on a copper core in 1965.

While a 10-cent coin was authorized, the coins never carried more than 10C to identify the denomination. The first were called "dismes" until 1837 when the official denomination on the coin became "dime." Like the half dimes, there are numerous varieties, with large- and small-date

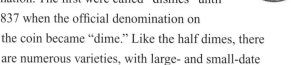

digits and 10C and overdates. The first ones carried the small eagle reverse and matched the half dimes.

The Roosevelt dime has been with us since 1946, honoring President Franklin D. Roosevelt and his connection with the March of Dimes for Polio. It made the transition from 90 percent silver to copper-nickel clad copper in 1965, although silver dimes dated 1964 were struck into 1966.

Proof dimes have received more than their share of attention, with several dates appearing with a missing "S" mintmark. Some 1982 circulation dimes also got out without a mintmark, the only known circulation date and denomination where this has happened. This also happened to some proof nickels and the 1990 no-S proof cent. These particular minting varieties are listed in most coin price guides.

Q:

Some years back there was a report that the San Francisco Mint was closed for a time because of a major embezzlement. Any facts you can offer?

A:

The arrest of a number of production employees for embezzlement of "coins, unstruck planchets, and purposely misstruck coins" occurred in March 1967. However, by 1970 things were back to "normal," and some pretty strange pieces - such as a 1970 dime struck on a 1933 New Mexico tax token - began turning up.

CHAPTER 30

20-CENT
DOUBLE
DIMES

At first glance, a 20-cent coin seems to be an oddball denomination, but it actually fits our decimal coinage. It's the 25-cent coin that really is a misfit.

The coin picked up its "double dime" nickname early on. Regardless of status, the coin simply was not popular and ended up on the scrap heap after a very brief appearance from 1875-1878.

The key coin of this series, both in numbers and values, is the 1876-CC that shows very strong hub doubling and has sold for as much as $148,500 for an MS-65 specimen and catalogs at $175,000 for a proof-65 specimen.

Q:
How did the Mint dispose of the 1,093,838,670 steel 1943 cents when they were removed from circulation?

A:
The Mint began withdrawal in 1945, and in 20 years retrieved 163 million, or about 14.9 percent of the steel cents in circulation. Some 900,000,000 are still out there.

CHAPTER 31

QUARTER
DOLLAR

The quarter dollar, or "quarter" as it is universally called, started as a 25-cent coin. Actually, the first quarters struck in 1796 didn't show a denomination. 25C was added in 1804 and lasted until 1838, replaced by "QUAR. DOL." The full wording wasn't spelled out until the Barber quarters of 1892.

Like the dime, production began with the small eagle reverse. The sequence of series was different following the Draped Bust, heraldic eagle. The Liberty Cap (1815-1828) design had "E PLURIBUS UNUM" above the eagle. It was removed in 1831 and the Seated Liberty design began in 1838.

Draped Bust Quarter,
Small Eagle

Draped Bust Quarter, Heraldic Eagle

Liberty Cap Quarter, E PLURIBUS UNUM above Eagle.

Liberty Cap Quarter, no banner above Eagle.

Q:

Wasn't the Board of Lady Managers responsible for the Isabella commemorative quarter struck for the 1892 Columbian Exposition unique in other ways?

A:

The claim was made in an article written by the head of the board, Mrs. Potter Palmer, in the June 1892 *Ladies Home Journal* that this was the first time in history that a body of women had been legally appointed to act in a national capacity for a government anywhere in the world.

The "no drapery" design lasted three years (1838-1840), followed by the "added drapery" variety used from 1840 on.

The "arrows at date" obverse lasted only three years – 1853-1855. The rays on the reverse – added at the same time – were removed in 1854. In 1866, the motto "IN GOD WE TRUST" appeared on a ribbon above the eagle. It remained, while the arrows were added to the date in 1871-1874 and removed again in 1875. Again, there was a slight reduction in weight for the earlier arrows and a slight increase in weight when they were removed.

Q:

I have a recent date clad coin that was struck with too small a core. The clad layers hang over the edges, but you can see the reeding on the smaller diameter core. How did this happen?

A:

You have an altered coin. The quarter has been dipped in acid, which cut down the core more rapidly than the rest of the coin, leaving a "slot" between the clad layers, but still showing the reeding on the edge of the copper core. As an altered coin it has no value.

Q:

Is there any record of who was responsible for putting George Washington on the quarter in 1932?

A:

U.S. Rep. Randolph Perkins of New Jersey apparently was the first to submit a bill in early 1931, which was passed by Congress on April 4, 1931. This resulted in the Washington commemorative of 1932.

The Barber quarters came along in 1892, succeeded by the Standing Liberty quarter (with TRVST like the later Peace dollar) in 1916.

The first Standing Liberty design in 1916 had Liberty's right breast exposed (not a wardrobe malfunction) but an intentionally classic design. The robe was closed in 1917 and the eagle was

moved up to make room for three stars. The quarter is replete with die varieties, making it a Mecca for collectors. Perhaps most famous is the 1918/1917-S overdate, one of several for the denomination, catalogued with a full head for $320,000. Full head refers to Liberty's head, showing all the detail. Most are flat as the design did not strike well.

The Washington quarter has been with us since 1932. It was intended to be a one-year circulating commemorative. However, unexpected public demand again affected production and the Mint resumed striking them in 1934.

In recent years the quarter has become the preferred coin of commerce. This leads us to today and the next chapter on the State quarters.

Q:
A friend of mine has an early Washington quarter with a crude swastika punched into it. Any idea as to the source?

A:
Back in the early days of World War II, before the United States got involved, the Treasury Department became aware of a small number of these coins found in circulation, apparently the work of a Nazi sympathizer. The perpetrator was considered to be a "screwball," who was defacing the coins with a screwdriver and a hammer.

CHAPTER 32

STATE
QUARTERS

The Royal Canadian Mint can take credit for an idea that has turned on millions of new collectors in the U.S. The U.S. Mint watched the popular success of the 1992 Canadian quarters honoring the 12 parts of the country from Alberta to the Yukon. It decided on an ambitious 50-coin program spread over 10 years to recognize each state in the Union.

Committees from each state selected the designs to be submitted to the Mint for a final selection. Several states allowed public voting on the designs.

Sales of the coins have been substantial. The Mint estimates that some 145 million people are collecting State quarters. Not just from their own state, but from every state that has a new coin.

However, some collectors carry a series like this too far, removing from circulation every state quarter they find. There are numerous collectors who have thousands of dollars tied up in the coins. You need only to look at the record amounts of bags and rolls being sold by the Mint.

The hard facts are that with so many collectors and the general public pulling them from circulation, there will be a surplus of these coins for decades to come. This applies mostly to those coins that have been in

circulation. The MS-65 and MS-67 grades are doing surprisingly well for a recent series.

For an object lesson you need only look at the Bicentennial coins, which went through the same collecting frenzy in 1976. The quarter still hasn't reached a $1 value for a 46-year old MS-60 grade specimen.

My standard advice is to collect only those coins you need to complete the series and to fill the family albums. Collect them in the best grade possible, preferably the highest possible uncirculated grade. Cash in 15 or 20 of the circulated coins and buy a MS-65 grade for your collection.

The state series began in 1999 and ended in 2008. Five state coins were struck each year by the Philadelphia mint and by the Denver mint. The mints are identified by a "P" or a "D" mintmark, located on the obverse of the coins directly below the "IN GOD WE TRUST" motto. All State quarters have the same obverse, with the bust of Washington facing left (the viewer's left).

The State quarters were issued in the order that the State entered the Union. I show the five for each year in that sequence:

1999

2000

2001

2002

2003

2004

2005

2006

2007

2008

Q:

What can you tell me about a coin I have that appears to be a mule of an Argentine coin and a U.S. quarter eagle gold coin?

A:

Were it not for the disappointment, I would be tempted to make a pun about "playing games." Sadly, this is no mule, but instead a game counter or poker chip, one of the American counters, as opposed to the multitude in use in Europe, and further one of three with similar obverses and the reverses of the $2.50, $5 and $10 gold coins. The pieces are brass or copper, without any precious metal content.

All five of the 1999 dates from both mints have been found with rotated reverses. If you turn a coin over, top to bottom, the reverse of the coin will be right side up, or "coin rotation." If the reverse is tilted, that's a rotated reverse. If it's upside down (180 degrees), that's "medal rotation." Rotated reverses of 45, 90 and 180 degrees are the most popular, in that order.

The Wisconsin coins have been found with extra leaves on the corn stalk and numerous New Hampshire coins have been reported with missing mintmarks, due to a filled die. These have value only in the uncirculated grades.

See! You've learned some history with your collection.

Q:
What is the significance of the dots and dashes around the edge of the Canadian 1943-45 5-cent reverse?

A:
It's International Morse Code, which differs on several letters from standard code. The dots and dashes translate as "We Win When We Work Willingly."

CHAPTER 33

D.C.
AND THE TERRITORIES

In 2009 the state quarter series was extended to include the District of Columbia and the Territories. Again there is a common obverse and each design was struck at both Philadelphia and Denver Note that there are six designs that were released in 2009, rather than the five per year for the State quarters.

A new series that will include state and national parks and monuments began in 2010. The releases will be much the same as the previous series.

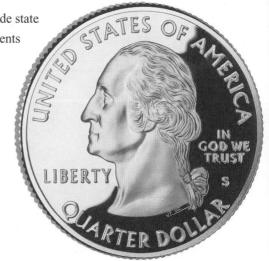

D.C. & THE TERRITORIES

CHAPTER 34

HALF
DOLLARS

Like the other denominations, the early half dollars (or halves) first struck in 1794 had a broad spectrum of die varieties. Large or small letters or digits, overdates and several different designs over the years give the half, which used to be a mainstay of commerce, a rich past. Like the half dime, the half dollar started with the Flowing Hair design (1794-1795), followed by the Draped Bust, small eagle (1796-1797) and the Draped Bust, heraldic eagle (1801-1807). In 1807, the Bust half with 50C was introduced, lasting until 1836, with a very lengthy list of overdates and other minting varieties. The design continued, but with "50 CENTS" spelled out (1836-1837).

For 1838-1839, the change was to "HALF DOL." The Seated Liberty series ran from 1839 to 1853 when arrows were added to the date along with rays around the eagle reverse. Like the quarter, the rays were removed in 1854 and the arrows disappeared in 1856.

In 1866, the ribbon with "IN GOD WE TRUST" was added above the eagle. The arrows came back

Q:

Aren't coin designs required by law to run for 25 years before they are changed?

A:

The law specifies a 25-year tenure for a design, but Congress has the power at any time to override the law by passing a special law with an exemption, which was the case with the Kennedy half and Ike dollar.

Q:

Was President Franklin
D. Roosevelt a coin
collector?

A:

His stamp collection
was better known, but
he did collect coins and
his collection was sold
several years after his
death.

for 1873-1874 and left again in 1875, again weight related.

Trust the mint reports in most catalogs; if they don't list a date or mint, it means there were no coins officially struck for that date or mint. If your coin is not listed it's likely to be either a counterfeit or have an altered date.

In 1892, the Barber design for the half took over. In 1916 the design was changed again to the Walking Liberty half. The mintmark appeared on the obverse, changed later in the year to the reverse. In 1948, Ben Franklin and a mini-eagle took their place.

In 1964, just months after he was assassinated, President John F. Kennedy replaced

Franklin. Like the other larger-denomination coins, the halves started with less than 90 percent silver before the long-term issue at that level.

When silver prices got out of control in the early 1960s, the rest of the coins turned to copper-nickel clad on copper cores, but the half dollar retained a 40 percent share of silver from 1965 through 1970 before joining the rest of the clad coins.

With the advent of the clad half dollars, the coin has disappeared from circulation, with the quarter becoming the de facto coin of commerce. Halves are still being struck, but primarily for collectors. Mintage figures are down sharply.

Since 1965, all of the denominations have at one time or another been minted in 40 percent or 90 percent silver. One type of proof set now carries 90 percent silver coins again.

CHAPTER 35

EARLY
DOLLARS

The silver dollars matched the first Flowing Hair design (1794-1795), the Draped Bust, small eagle (1796-1798), Draped Bust, heraldic eagle (1798-1804), Seated Liberty, no motto (1840-1866), and the Seated Liberty with "IN GOD WE TRUST" above the eagle (1866-1873).

The old silver dollars were just about the most unloved coins in our pockets, except in small areas in the west and south. The new, small-size Anthony and Sacagawea dollars are just about the most unloved coins in our pockets today. Get the picture? The public does not like and even hates a dollar coin.

Q:
Didn't a Mint official once make a flat statement that no more dollars would ever be produced?

A:
Mint Director George E. Roberts on June 30, 1904, said: "There will never be another silver dollar minted in this country."

CHAPTER 36

TRADE
DOLLARS

The Mint stopped producing standard silver dollars from 1874 to 1877. Beginning in 1873 the U.S. Mint struck Trade dollars for use in the Orient. The last Trade dollars were struck in 1884 under a black cloud of scandal. Unfortunately, the U.S. Mint and Congress have several times ignored history.

The Trade dollars were struck to different specifications, intended to break the strangle hold on Oriental trade by the Mexican peso. The specs were part of the design, stating: "420 GRAINS .900 FINE." The standard dollar weighed 416 grains, given in most price guides as 26.7300 grams.

The new coins were accepted and promptly chop marked with various designs representing traders and banks. The coins were given legal tender status until 1876, but high silver prices brought millions of the coins back to the U.S. Legal tender status was finally restored by the Coinage Act of 1965. Today, coins without chop marks rate a premium.

Q:
Did the Mint refer to proof coins as medals?

A:
There are several instances of this, including the subterfuge of selling the Trade dollar proofs as medals to get around the Treasury Department order halting production of the Trade dollar in 1878.

CHAPTER 37

MORGAN
DOLLARS

In 1878 the Morgan dollar was introduced with mintages ranging to hundreds of millions of dollars. The first ones were called Bland dollars, after U.S. Rep. Richard P. "Silver Dick" Bland, who had a hand in originating them. They were also called Buzzard dollars, or Daddy dollars. The former was a disparaging comment on the eagle and the latter was a reference to the dollars that our forefathers used. Later the naming referred to George T. Morgan, who designed the coin.

Large numbers of the Morgans are still around. Several major hordes were uncovered in the years after the last Morgans were struck. Almost any coin dealer will sell you a bag of 1,000 Morgan dollars.

The series started off with three important varieties centered on the arrows in the eagle's claws. As a multitude of other varieties occurred, Leroy Van Allen and George Mallis began cataloging them, assigning VAM numbers to each variety. This system brought to light many fascinating deviations and became a major factor in collecting the Morgans.

The series was struck in every year, some at four mints, including Philadelphia, San Francisco, New Orleans and Carson City, ending in 1904. After a 13-year gap, the last of the Morgans were struck in 1921 at Denver, Philadelphia and San Francisco.

Q:

It's my understanding that President Hayes didn't want the Morgan dollar struck. Is that correct?

A:

Hayes vetoed the bill ordering the striking of the coin in 1878, but Congress passed it over his veto, and then rubbed it in by having the first coin struck presented to the unwilling President.

CHAPTER 38

PEACE
DOLLARS

Peace dollars were struck beginning in 1921. The nickname came from the word "PEACE" on the lower reverse. Just over a million were struck that year, but the flood gates opened in 1922, with a mintage of over 81 million from San Francisco, Denver and Philadelphia, the largest single year and the most commonly found examples today.

The Peace dollars lasted officially until 1935, but 1964-D dollars were struck with the Peace design and then destroyed. Rumors still circulate that a handful escaped the melting pot. The key coin for the series is the 1928-S (Large S), cataloging at $29,500 in MS-65.

Q:

The Treasury went to a lot of expense to promote circulation of the Anthony dollar. Any other such promotion?

A:

On a somewhat smaller scale, the Treasury resorted to several gimmicks to promote circulation of the Peace dollar. One of the schemes tried was to put a silver dollar into the pay envelopes of each of the 5,000 Treasury employees. Before admitting defeat the Treasury had managed to "push" $10,000,000 into circulation, but in a matter of months they were back in the vaults.

CHAPTER 39

EISENHOWER
'IKE'
DOLLARS

Just when we thought we'd seen the last of the big dollars, Congress decided to honor President Dwight D. Eisenhower with his own dollar. Faced with rising silver prices, the decision was made in 1971 to go with two versions – proof and special uncirculated – that only contained 40 percent silver, while the circulating coins were copper-nickel clad. The public turned thumbs down as thousands hoarded what they assumed to be silver, since the coins were frequently mislabeled as "silver" dollars.

The Ike design, especially the world map on the reverse, reveals what Chief Engraver Frank Gasparro admitted to as "tinkering" with the dies. He used more than 40 different working hubs for the series, including the notorious "Peg Leg" Ikes that had no serifs on the left leg of the R in "AMERICA." As adverse as I am to nicknames, I couldn't resist tagging this one, and the nickname stuck. Although you will probably never see one, the Ikes are still legally in circulation. The end of production came in 1978. For the last two years the design reverted to the pre-1976 reverse.

Q:

The original authorization for the Ike dollars included 150 million silver coins. They didn't even come close did they?

A:

Not by a country mile. Between 1971 and 1974 the Mint struck only about 21 million 40 percent silver Ikes.

Q:

Were all of the 40 percent silver Ike dollars produced under the same law?

A:

The 1971-S through 1974-S 40 percent silver Ikes were struck under the provisions of the original Ike dollar Coinage Act of 1970, while the 1976-S dollars, as well as the 40 percent halves and quarters, were struck under the provisions of the Bicentennial Coinage Act of 1973.

CHAPTER 40

SUSAN B. ANTHONY
DOLLARS

"If big doesn't work, then downsize." That sentiment came out as the few Ikes in circulation faded away. The result was a coin midway in size between the quarter and the half dollar. Susan B. Anthony took the honors of being grimly featured on the obverse.

The public reaction was to be expected. Messing with the size only added to the problems as the first coins hit the street in 1979. The coins were spent as quarters because of the slight size difference, resulting in unpleasant losses and even worse language. The lesson not learned – the public did not want a dollar coin, of any size.

For collectors, the coin was entertaining and profitable. The 1979

date came with a near date or far date, depending on the distance from the rim. One caution, the width of the rim is not a valid marker, despite its frequent use. Wide or narrow rims are found on both the near and far date coins.

The big news was my discovery that two different mintmarks had been used for the 1979 proofs, during a visit to the San Francisco Mint. The original "blob" mintmark on the proof coins was replaced with a symmetrical S, which had perfect circle upper and lower loops.

This Type II mintmark became the Type I for the 1981-S proofs, replaced in the midst of the 1981 proof coin production with an "S" with a perfect circle lower loop and an elongated and flattened upper loop.

Except for the varieties, most SBA dollars went straight from the bank to businesses to customers and straight back to the bank.
The authorization was still in effect, so when the vaults were nearly empty, they struck the last SBA dollars in 1999.

Q:
I have a proof SBA dollar that looks like it is made of gold. Is this possible?

A:
Very probably your coin is one of the thousands that were plated by a commercial firm and sold as souvenirs. The plating makes the piece an altered coin, so it has no collector value. The gold is worth only a few cents.

Q:
Didn't the post offices and the Army get involved in trying to make the SBA dollars circulate?

A:
The post offices across the country were enlisted, and passed out large quantities of the coins, but the effort only delayed the inevitable trip back to the bank. The Defense Department tried to force service personnel stationed in Europe to use the coins in place of paper dollars, but the experiment collapsed because most foreign countries will not exchange their currencies for coins.

CHAPTER 41

SACAGAWEA
DOLLARS

The Sacagawea dollars were struck beginning in 2000. The only happy people were the collectors who have made the silver Peace and Morgan dollars one of the most popular collectibles.

There is a famous quote: "Those who ignore history are forced to repeat it."

If you are thinking that this foolishness is over and done with, think again. They tried a new alloy for the Sac dollars – copper, zinc, manganese and nickel – which gave them a golden color. The Mint touted them as "golden dollars," but the public heard it as "gold dollars," with resultant confusion.

The Sac dollars were issued from 2000 to 2005, went away for three years and returned with new reverses in 2009 and 2010. As the TV pitchmen say, "But we're not done yet."

Q:

How did the Mint count its coins before the invention of the mechanical counting machines?

A:

Mechanical counting machines were not introduced at the Mint until some time after 1900. Before that it was strictly a hand counting job, with the help of what was called a counting board. This was a flat board, made for each denomination with copper partitions separated by the diameter of the coin. The boards were designed so that when each row was filled, the total would be some even amount.

CHAPTER 42

PRESIDENTIAL
DOLLARS

Someone came up with the bright idea of doing a series of dollars with portraits of the U.S. Presidents, as if this had not been done before with U.S. Mint medals. As expected, George Washington led the parade. The plan is to issue four a year, beginning in 2007:

2007

2007

2008

2009

2010

CHAPTER 43

GOLD
COINS

Gold coins were the mainstay of our economy from the very beginning of our nation. Although all but the smallest denominations were beyond the reach of the average person, banks used them as assets. Gold was discovered in a number of places and much of it was converted to coinage.

Most of the public didn't need gold coins in a period when a $5 or $10 gold coin was a month's wages. The banks got the most benefit – assets that were compact and easily stored. A good argument could be made that there was only a very limited need for gold coins, other than the banks, and the prestige of having a gold currency.

CHAPTER 44

$1 GOLD

The $1 gold was first struck in 1849 with the Type 1 Liberty Head. The Indian Head or Type 2 (Small Head) was struck from 1854-1856, and was replaced by the Type 3 Indian Head, (Large Head) last struck in 1889. The gold dollars were unpopular because of their small size. There really was no need for a gold dollar, since there were ample supplies of silver dollars. The public disaffection with the two coins was repeated with the SBA dollars and the Ike dollars, as well as the Sac and Presidential dollars.

CHAPTER 45

$2.50 GOLD

The $2.50 gold was struck beginning in 1796 as the Liberty Cap. In 1808, the Turban Head appeared, modified in 1809 with stars above the smaller head. In 1829, the diameter was reduced. The Classic Head appeared in 1834 with a reduction in fineness. The Coronet Head (1840-1907) settled on .900 fine. The Indian Head was struck from 1908 to 1929.

Congress settled on the $10 denomination defined as an eagle. This made the $2.50 gold a quarter eagle.

$3 GOLD

Like the gold dollar, the $3 gold didn't fit the Eagle denominations. The $3 gold was intended to pay for a sheet of 100 3-cent stamps. Other uses were found and the coin was struck from 1854 to 1889.

$5 GOLD
HALF EAGLES

The $5 half eagle began with the Liberty Cap and small or heraldic eagle in 1795. The Turban Head Capped Draped Bust replaced it in 1807 and in turn was followed by the Turban Head Capped Head in 1813, the Classic Head in 1834 and the Coronet Head in 1839. "IN GOD WE TRUST" was added on a ribbon above the eagle in 1866. The Indian Head took over in 1908 and was struck until 1929. Production of gold Eagles and fractional Eagles resumed as bullion coins in 1986 and commemoratives in 1984.

Q:

Q:
Who gets the credit for the "IN GOD WE TRUST" motto on our currency?

A:
The Rev. Mark Richards Watkinson of Pennslyvania wrote Secretary of the Treasury Salmon P. Chase in 1861 suggesting "God, Liberty, Law." Chase agreed to the idea, but it was not made law until July 11, 1955.

CHAPTER 48

$10 GOLD
EAGLES

The $10 gold eagle started with the small eagle in 1795-1797. The eagle was officially named in 1795 and continues with the other gold denominations to the present day. In sequence came the heraldic eagle (1797-1804), Old Coronet Head (1838-1839), New Coronet Head (1839-1866), and continuing with the added "IN GOD WE TRUST" to 1907. The motto was removed in 1907 and restored in 1908 with production until 1933.

Q:

Is there a dollar value placed on the gold coins that were surrendered to the Treasury following their recall in 1933 and 1934?

A:

Mint figures show that $1,933,809,000 in gold coins were withdrawn and melted under the provisions of the various regulations established in 1933. This included $1.329 billion face value in double eagles and $177.3 million in eagles, the rest the smaller denominations.

In 1933, President Roosevelt used an Executive Order to call in gold and Gold Certificates, but only a fraction of the outstanding gold was recovered.

Since then, gold has again become legal to own and the U.S. Mint regularly issues gold bullion coins.

CHAPTER 49

$20 GOLD
DOUBLE EAGLES

Like the $1 gold, the $20 gold double eagle didn't start until 1849, with one known for that year. In part of 1861, a different Anthony C. Paquet reverse was used, creating another rarity. The Longacre reverse was resumed in 1862. "IN GOD WE TRUST" was added in 1866. In 1877, the "TWENTY D." was changed to "TWENTY DOLLARS."

In 1907-1908, the motto was removed, returning in 1909. The Saint-Gaudens design was used from 1907 to 1933. The one official survivor of the 1933 mintage sold in 2002 for $7,590,000.

Today, gold coins are expensive collectibles, even though many can be bought for little more than the melt value of the coins. It's the melt value that keeps the cost up. Gold is a popular investment. However, don't jump in before you read the chapter on investments. Close your checkbook and sit on it, firmly.

Q:
I have a Blake & Co. $20 piece that appears to be gold. It pictures a coin press and has an incuse 20 on it. What is it worth?

A:
I'm sorry to disappoint you, but you have a very common copy of an early California piece. The Chrysler Corporation had scores of thousands of the copies (brass) of the $20 gold coin made in 1969 to promote the introduction of the 1970 Plymouth Gold Duster Valiant. They are a perennial problem for collectors.

CHAPTER 50

BULLION
COINS

Striking gold, silver and platinum bullion coins has become big business for several world mints, especially South Africa, Austria and Canada, as well as the United States. They are legal tender with a denomination stated on the coin. Since each coin contains substantially more bullion value than the stated denomination, nobody would spend them at face value.

Let me hedge on that statement. There are always a few lost souls who are unaware of this little bit of trickery. There is ample anecdotal evidence that someone who was hard up or had just stolen them, would try and exchange them for something since they might have no idea of their real worth.

You would expect that they are not collector coins, but it didn't work out that way. I have been told personally of lengthy searches through stacks of American Eagles in an effort to find examples in the upper five grades, (MS-66-70 or PR-66-70) which in turn can be sold for a substantial premium.

Bullion coins are struck on nearly pure metal, at least .999 fine in most cases. The Royal Canadian Mint made a big splash by going to "four nines" or .9999. The difference between three or four nines is microscopic, but it was a good marketing ploy and other mints have followed suit. Even the hucksters tout their gold plated tokens as having .9999 fine plating.

Silver American Eagles come only in the $1 denomination and are larger in diameter than the old silver dollars. The silver is 0.9993 fine.

As this is being written, gold is well over $1,000, which puts the $50 gold coins (1 ounce) out of the reach of many collectors and even many investors, who have been flocking to gold as an inflation hedge. However, there also are 1/10 ($5), 1/4 ($10) and 1/2 ounce ($25) gold bullion coins. All four are 0.9167 fine. The silver and gold Eagles were first produced in 1986 and the platinum bullion coins were first struck in 1997.

Platinum denominations are the 1/10 ($10), 1/4 ($25), 1/2 ounce ($50) and 1 ounce ($100). All are 0.9995 fine. Most were struck at West Point.

The Bison bullion coinage began with the 2008-W $5, $10 and $25. The $50 gold series began in 2006, again at West Point. This series has the Indian facing right, with the buffalo facing left.

The First Spouse coins, honoring the wives of the Presidents are $10 gold with a half ounce of gold, struck at West Point. This is one of two weights for the $10 gold. The original Eagles (1838-1933) contained slightly less than half an ounce. The current American Eagle and Buffalo coins contain a quarter of an ounce. The old $10 fineness was also used for commemoratives in 1984 and 2003.

Q:
Is 100 percent pure silver possible?

A:
Only in a lab. Usually the best you can get is .9999 fine, which means it has a trace of impurities.

Q:
What do the abbreviations ASW and AGW stand for?

A:
Actual silver weight or actual gold weight. There's a third one — APW — for actual platinum weight. In all three cases the figure refers to the actual weight of the bullion metal, not the total weight of the coin.

This would be a good place to remind you that prices for bullion coins rise and fall, usually lagging the actual market, but you can get a general idea from the daily spot price listings.

The big fad of the 1970s was the collecting of silver art bars and rounds. Most contained an ounce of silver, with a few multiples. At least one large catalog was produced listing most of the existing bars and rounds. The bars had a multitude of different designs, hence the art bar label. When silver shot to $52 an ounce in 1980, many of the bars and rounds headed for the smelter. The multitude of private mints disappeared right along with the silver.

This would be a good place to remind you that prices for bullion coins rise and fall, usually lagging the actual market, but you can get a general idea from the daily spot price listings. They are printed in big city newspapers and are readily available from the Internet.

CHAPTER 51

YOUR HEIRS

You are never too young to make a will. The odds of getting run over by a bus or having a heart attack at a tender age are slim, but these events do happen. Even for younger readers, it won't hurt to do some planning. If you don't plan, very bad things can happen. A lot of people don't want to talk about, or even think about their demise, but it's a fact of life.

From personal experience, I can tell you that things go much smoother with advance plans in place. If there is nobody in your family who is interested in coins, you can't just toss your collection in the air to fall where it may. The best thing to do is bequeath it to a friend – the guy you've swapped coins with for years. If that doesn't work, consider donating it to your local coin club, or to the ANA for a tax credit. The local club undoubtedly can use your reference library. If there are some rare and valuable books, donate them to the ANA.

Don't leave anything to chance and don't walk away muttering, "It's not my problem. Let them fight it out." Believe me, they will.

Don't will or give your coin collection or your reference books to

Q:
I've discovered I have several coins with what appears to be engraving on the coins. Are these altered coins?

A:
Work on the coin is an alteration, commonly referred to as "tooling." Many old time collections contain Indian Head cents with the diamonds tooled, and the chest feathers of the eagle on the Morgan dollars are often tooled. At the time this was an accepted practice, but this is no longer the case and a tooled coin will be severely discounted.

a charity or church, as most have no facility – or the necessary knowledge – to handle a collection and most likely will recover only a fraction of its real worth. If, God forbid, your heirs are likely to get into a squabble over your estate, then designate exactly who you want to give or sell the coins to, or who should auction them off, so that the monetary proceeds can be divided according to your will. This is far better than trying to divide the coins equally.

Expect a fight over your assets and you probably will be right. Forestall as much of the rancor as possible by leaving explicit instructions for the disposal of your collection. Put your specific instructions with your collection. Give your lawyer or the potential executor of your estate copies and make them part of your will. Don't leave anything to chance and don't walk away muttering, "It's not my problem. Let them fight it out." Believe me, they will. That's how lawyers make a plush living. Don't forget that list of the coins with the prices you paid for them. The IRS is waiting.

CHAPTER 52

COIN DEALERS

Coin price guides mostly quote retail prices for coins. This is because dealers use wholesale prices and add their individual markup, so no two dealers are likely to have the same retail prices. Coin dealers won't give you

wholesale prices, but they may give a small discount if you look like a good customer.

When buying, use your senses. Look at the coin, preferably with a magnifier. Listen to what the dealer is saying about it. Since you already know a lot about the coin, you can compare the sales pitch with reality. Stop if the deal doesn't meet your criteria. In other words, "Stop, look and listen." Or, to put it another way: "Look and listen, then Stop, or Go."

When you do find a dealer that meets your standards, hang on to him or her. The more business you do, the more you are likely to profit from buying. Most dealers are happy to share their expertise with regular customers.

Until you are expert in all areas of your collection, I would avoid buying "sight unseen" coins. This is the quickest way to the Poor Farm. Especially

Q:
I see lots of offers to sell coins but none to buy. Where are the buyers?

A:
Show me a coin dealer who can sell coins without buying them to replenish his stock and I'll show you a miracle worker. Every dealer sooner or later has to replace the coins that are sold so this is one of the numismatic facts of life. If a dealer runs an ad offering coins, it is implied that he also buys similar coins.

wait until you have lots of experience before getting into Internet auctions. A seller's high rating doesn't necessarily mean you will get an accurately graded, problem-free coin.

Before buying that beautiful coin offered on TV, try the local coin dealers. In most cases, they can provide the same coin at a fraction of the cost. When you sell, expect offers that are discounted heavily from the retail value, unless the coin is especially valuable, or one the dealer needs for a client.

Many collectors make the mistake of expecting full retail from a dealer. Like any other business, the coin dealer has to buy at wholesale in order to profit on a retail sale to pay the help, rent, taxes and other expenses of doing business.

Don't expect dealers to reward you for spending hours going through circulated coins. Despite the prices listed in price guides, the average dealer has no use for rolls of circulated clad quarters, halves and dimes, or nickels and cents. The dealer has no market, since anyone with time on their hands can search rolls of coins. What this boils down to is that – except for the odd silver coin that shows up – you should spend the coins, rather than keeping them for a dreamed of day when a dealer wants them.

Collectively there are probably millions of dollars worth of coins that are being hoarded – both by collectors and the public – based on the assumption that they will gain in value as they get older. The assumption is based in part on fact, but any appreciation will be painfully slow. It will be even slower than the better choice – a savings account. The important thing to remember is that in nearly all cases uncirculated grade coins will appreciate much more quickly than coins that are worn.

Most price guides show the retail value of the coin, usually in several grades. This is confusing to the novice, who assumes that is the price someone will pay for the coin. The important point to understand is that the retail price is a base. Every dealer deducts his or her profit margin from the retail figure, just as every other business does. Be happy that coin dealers don't use the really complicated formulas that are used in other instances.

Don't make the mistake of trying to sell your coins by putting an ad in the local newspaper. You are asking to get your coins hijacked, even if you meet your potential customers in a bank. It's unsafe at any speed. Most local coin clubs have swap meets or auctions where you are likely to do better and be in a safe environment.

Many "vest pocket" dealers offer coins for sale in the hobby publications classified sections, but I'll remind you that until you can grade for yourself, you need to be careful of the offers. In the event you do have a problem with a classified or display ad seller, publications have a person who serves as a consumer advocate, who can be of help in getting things straightened out.

You will need every bit of the paper trail, a log of phone calls or e-mail messages and any other

Q:
What is meant by a dealer's ad offering "un-searched coins?" How can it be un-searched if the dealer guarantees that it contains a specific key coin as is typically done?

A:
Dealers usually don't have the time to go through very many coins. To fulfill their promise they just open the top of the bag and dump the key coin in, which takes no time at all. It really has no bearing on the other coins in the bag.

Q:
What is a PDS Set?

A:
It's a set of coins from the Philadelphia, Denver and San Francisco Mints, most often a mint-packaged mint set consisting of all the coins struck at the three Mints for a given year. The old timers called it a PSD set, listing the Mints in the order in which they began striking coins.

When selling a collection, sell the coins as a group. Don't let anyone "cherry pick" the collection by buying the valuable coins and leaving the lower valued pieces behind.

evidence that will be helpful, such as a listing by issue date and the page number of the ad you responded to. The more pertinent information you have, the more likely you will get a successful settlement.

When selling a collection, sell the coins as a group. Don't let anyone "cherry pick" the collection by buying the valuable coins and leaving the lower valued pieces behind. Make a list of your coins, showing exactly what you paid for each one. If you cannot show proof you paid a premium for a coin, the IRS will take the difference between the sale price and the face value of the coin as taxable profit. Picture what that does to a $20 gold piece. Copy this paragraph and post it where you can't miss it.

When selling, take your list and a few sample coins and shop them to several dealers to find the one with the most interest in your collection. If it is a large or valuable collection, you will want to find an appraiser to give you an idea of the value before you try to sell it. Here again, the list comes in handy.

Coin dealers have had a bad rap. The public perception of coin dealers ranks them down close to used-car salesmen. This is an unfair assessment, due mainly to the fact that the public knows next to nothing about coin collecting. Their only contact probably was to try and sell some coins. Or they may have heard of a neighbor's "bad deal."

Word of mouth is great advertising for a firm, but it can never catch up with bad mouthing. While there are a few bad apples in the bunch, the majority of coin dealers are like any retailer, hard-working assets to the community. Show me a business that doesn't have some sinners, but the coin dealers continue to take it in the neck. I even get grumbles because dealers are charging prices over face value for "government owned" coins.

A big part of the problem is the misconception that coin dealers somehow differ from all other businesses that pay wholesale prices for the merchandise they sell at retail. Many collectors get furious when they are offered a discounted price for their coins. They display their ignorance of common business practices by this attitude and the result is unwarranted bad press for the dealer.

The solution is to realize that buying and selling coins is, in fact, a business and it will not survive if there is no profit. You, in turn, have several ways to ensure that you are not being ripped off. It's a good idea when doing business with a dealer you are unfamiliar with to first make several small purchases or sales.

Questions to ask yourself include, "Was the dealer courteous? Did he know his stock? Was the coin accurately graded? Were you satisfied with the cost?"

Q:

Could you explain how one date on a coin can be 'better' than another?

A:

The question arises from seeing the term 'better dates' in ads in the hobby publications. It's a sort of dealer shorthand, meaning that a "better" date is one of the lower mintage dates or a more popular date with collectors, in contrast to the common dates.

Q:

What should I do about an overcharge on my credit card?

A:

If you have been overcharged, the seller is the SECOND call you should make. The first call should be to notify your credit card company immediately. DO NOT wait for the dealer to correct it, as you have to notify the card company within 120 days or there is no way to recover the money. By the time you receive your card company bill the matter is out of the seller's hands anyway.

If the dealer passes the test you've found a good place to do business on a larger scale. This is the same thing you would do when buying anything. What's different between buying a coin or going into a hardware store and buying a pound of nails? Or going to a grocery store? Coin prices fluctuate. So does the price of grapes or bananas. The grocer buys from the producer at wholesale and sells at retail.

Once you see the coin dealer as a business person, you will have come a long way toward a successful relationship with the dealer.

It will surprise you, but one of the biggest problems that dealers have are collectors trying to rip them off in any of a hundred ways, not limited to the thief who stuffs his pockets with coins when the dealer isn't looking or is taking care of a legitimate customer. That's one reason why you see heavy security at coin shows.

Coin dealers realize that they are prime targets not only for sneak thieves, but also for organized gangs that often trail a dealer leaving a show until he stops for gas or food. In a matter of seconds, these practiced robbers can break open car trunks, cut chains or break windows to get at coins inside the car, leaving the scene before the dealer even has a chance to react. As a result, dealers with high-end coins are turning to the armored-car services to get them safely to and from a show.

If you are seen making big purchases at a show, the same thing could happen to you, so exercise more than the usual care to ensure you aren't being followed in the show and when you leave.

Show security is a major process. That's why you are required to wear a name badge while you are at the show. At a large show, there are multiples of millions of dollars in coins and paper money, so they naturally want to make sure the people prowling the floor are legitimate attendees. At large shows there will be an armed police officer at the door and others stationed around the room, along with plainclothes officers or guards roaming the floor. Remember, they are there for your protection. Don't interfere with their duties.

One last piece of advice. If there is a disturbance on the show floor, don't rush over to gawk. If a shot were fired, you could easily be the accidental target. You won't see them, but a number of coin dealers provide their own protection with a gun close at hand. Don't let your natural curiosity get you into a bad situation.

When you've been to a dealer's shop or a show and purchased coins, don't leave them on the seat of your car. The best place is in the trunk until you get to the bank where you keep your coins or some other safe place. Always be alert to anyone near you as you approach your car. Hit the door-lock switch as you enter the car to foil a car-jacker. Be security conscious at all times.

Q:
There's a poem about silver dollars. Do you know it?

A:
There are others, but this is one I do know:

Oh give me a big silver dollar, to throw on the bar with a bang.
A dollar all creased may do in the East, but we like our money to clang.

CHAPTER 53

JOIN
A COIN CLUB

No matter what level you are at – novice, intermediate, expert or veteran – you will be well served if you join a coin club. If there isn't one in your city, then start one! The American Numismatic Association has free literature on starting a club, including a sample set of by-laws and a Constitution. All you have to do is ask.

Local coin clubs are really the backbone of the hobby. This is where the novice begins to learn from other members or from educational "Show and Tell" exhibits. Most clubs have a speaker putting on a program. If you are worried about security, so are the other members, so you have a common problem, but one that will not leave the room. Think security at all times.

Coin clubs are found at local, state, regional, national and international levels. Each has its own purpose. The state and regional clubs often have local clubs as members, with the locals sharing the information and expertise of the higher club.

Many of the regional and national clubs are specialist clubs, devoted to one particular portion of the hobby, such as the Token and Medal Society (TAMS), the Civil War Token Society (CWTS) or the Combined

Organization of Numismatic Error Collectors of America (CONECA).

At the top of the international list is the 29,000-member American Numismatic Association (ANA), which has been around since 1891. Even older is the American Numismatic Society. The ANA is chartered by Congress and has more than 500 local, regional and national clubs as members. Its mantra is education. It has a wide range of educational services, including the ever-expanding Summer Seminars as well as the largest numismatic museum and largest numismatic library in the country. I'm proud to have served on the ANA Board of Governors.

If there's a numismatic collectible, there's probably a club devoted to it. If you are on the Internet, you can reach the ANA list of member clubs at www.money.org. Many of the clubs have their own Web sites.

For the beginning collector, I strongly urge you to join a local club, with an eye on joining the ANA and any regional or national club that matches your collecting interests. Dues for most clubs are quite reasonable. One of the better examples is the Mesa Coin Club in Arizona, which offers a life membership for $5 as long as you attend at least one meeting in a calendar year.

A suggestion I've been making in programs I've done recently for local clubs is to start a mentoring program. List each club member's specialties. When a new member comes in, assign him or

Q:
One of the coins in my new mint set has deep parallel indentations in the rims on both sides. How did this happen?

A:
This is a packaging damage, caused by the coin being out of place so that the sealing jaws, which form the compartments in the plastic envelope, closed on the coin rims. Contact the Mint for a replacement.

Q:

I've noted a number of ads for coins, offering "dates of our choice." Is this some sort of scam? I want to pick my own dates, not have someone do it for me and charge me for the privilege.

A:

The offer of "dates of our choice" is a perfectly legitimate offer that is frequently made, directed toward the individual who is interested in a type coin, as opposed to a coin of a specific date and mint.

her to the club member with the same or similar specialties as a mentor. The new member has a lot to learn and the specialists have a lot of knowledge they can share.

You may get a negative reaction from some of the club members, especially those that avoid any work. However, the point to bring across is that every collector is a specialist at some level. Literally anyone who knows two facts is way ahead of the one-fact person and miles ahead of the no-fact person. That's why your club members are considered to be specialists.

It's far better in a one-on-one situation, but I've been mentoring collectors by mail and e-mail for many years. I've read almost all of the books in my reference library, so I'm classed as an expert in several areas. My question-and-answer columns have reached many thousands of collectors with new knowledge and my books are reaching thousands more. You don't have to be a successful author to be a mentor, but it helps.

Local clubs often have a lending library of hobby publications and books. This is a good place to begin, and if your club doesn't have a library, start one. It's as simple as bringing a box of books to the meetings.

CHAPTER 54

RESOURCES TO HELP YOU
COLLECT

This is one of those "Where to Start?" chapters. There are literally hundreds of resources available. One is the ANA's Dwight Manley Library, which with more than 50,000 books, is the largest numismatic library in the country. ANA, not so incidentally, is the largest numismatic organization in the world. The nice thing is that it is a lending library, so ANA members can borrow almost any book just by paying the postage. Non-members can also borrow books, but they have to go through the Inter-Library system at their local library. The ANA library also fields research questions, but be warned that there is a $35-an-hour fee for extensive research.

There are lots of publications. Krause Publications, a division of F+W Media, has no less than five separate magazines and newspapers – *Coins* magazine, *Coin Prices* magazine, *Numismatic News* (The oldest coin hobby publication), *World Coin News* and *Bank Note*

Q:

Why are mintage figures missing or incomplete, especially when two different series are involved?

A:

Chalk this up to government style bookkeeping. It was centered strictly on numbers struck, ignoring two or more different designs or dates used in the same period. In the early days two or three dates might be struck in the same year.

Reporter. My "Clinic" columns appear in all but *Coin Prices*. In addition, there are numerous price guides, books and catalogs covering the broad spectrum of numismatics. You can find them – with excerpts – on the Internet at: www.shopnumismaster.com.

Several other publishers offer competing books, magazines and newspapers. It undoubtedly will surprise even some of the old timers to learn that there is a substantial amount of competition in the hobby publishing business. Price guides are a typical example. Protecting a heavy investment in pricing information is a constant struggle, especially when someone comes along and says, "Why don't you get your prices from (another publication)." Not only would it be a copyright violation, but since there is a legion of specialists providing us with pricing information, we believe we have the more accurate pricing information.

Evidence of the lack of comprehension is the next guy that comes along and says, "Your price is way off from so-and-so, so you need to correct it." Once someone has convinced themselves of the 'truth," no amount of arguing is going to help point out that just perhaps so-and-so is wrong and not us.

A number of coin dealers also send out publications ranging from flyers to multi-page magazines. Many of the coin clubs have monthly or quarterly publications. The ANA publishes the monthly *The Numismatist* as a membership benefit, with articles on a wide array of numismatic topics. A recent change in the membership reduces the dues if you use the online publication rather than getting the paper copies.

Most auction houses also issue color catalogs for their sales. Coin price guides come in all hues. Krause contributes *North American Coins and Prices*, which lists Canadian and Mexican coins besides the U.S. coins. It also has a dozen chapters devoted to all phases of coin collecting. Also from Krause is the annual *U.S. Coin Digest*.

This list could go on and on, but with limited space we need to aim you in the right direction to find answers for yourself. I answer questions on the Internet and there are several clubs and commercial sources that you can find on the Net.

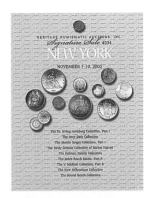

Learn how to use one of the search engines on the Internet. It's relatively easy and you'll be amazed at the amount of information you can find. I'm getting an increasing number of questions that could have been answered by a five minute search on the Internet. If you use the advanced section of Google, you'll no doubt be astounded by the speed with which hundreds or even thousands of pages related to your topic are found.

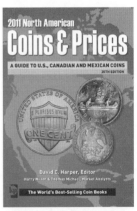

Ask lots of questions. I'll be glad to answer them, or refer you to one of the specialists in that particular area. You can reach me on the Internet at AnswerMan2@aol.com.

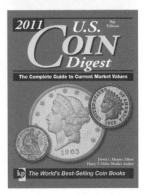

CHAPTER 55

Your Coin Collecting

LIBRARY

Your numismatic library can be as large or small as you choose. If you are a typical collector, you may have a price guide and perhaps one or two other books. If you are a smart collector, you will have at least one bookcase shelf full. You will need as a minimum, the following:

1. An up-to-date price guide.
2. A grading guide.
3. A detailed explanation of the minting process.
4. A subscription to one or more of the hobby publications.
5. A specialty club membership that includes a publication.
6. Any available books on your specialty or collecting interest.
7. A numismatic dictionary or encyclopedia.

I'm not suggesting that you get all of them immediately, but I do recommend that you budget for their purchase, along with the tools and coins that you are collecting. You can establish your own priorities as to when you acquire them. As your library grows, you will undoubtedly add reference material from other areas of the hobby.

There will be new books published that you will want. It's a hard choice to make, deciding whether to buy a book or a coin, but the benefits of the book will be long term. Be sure that when you work out your hobby budget for the year, you include money for subscriptions, club dues, tools and supplies, and reference books, along with your coins. The four expenditures will give you the largest possible return and the biggest bang for your buck. Don't forget travel expenses if you plan on attending a coin show in another city.

Once you begin to understand the benefits you will realize that you actually are investing in knowledge. Once you have the knowledge, it will earn dividends with every coin you add to your collection.

By now you more fully realize the complexities of the coin hobby. I've been able to barely scratch the surface, but there are tons of information and advice out there waiting for you to come along. It takes work, but there is satisfaction at the end of the tunnel that you probably couldn't find in any other way.

I'm not trying to scare you away by making things too complicated. I'm trying to help you avoid some of the pitfalls and traps that are always out there. You can participate at any level that suits you because it's your collection, not one belonging to the pundits.

Q:
Why was a weight of 48 grains picked for the small cent?

A:
Two reasons are quoted. One is that many of the Civil War tokens were of this average weight. The second is that this is exactly 1/10th of a troy ounce, even though copper, tin and zinc were never weighed (outside of the Mint) to this standard.

CHAPTER 56

Going to a Coin
Show

If you are fortunate enough to live in or near a fairly large city, there is likely to be a coin show nearby. Reader surveys at F+W Media indicate that the average collector is willing to drive up to 200 miles to get to a show. Really serious collectors might drive several hundred miles beyond that or fly to a distant show. What's the attraction?

That's a question with several answers. The biggest selling point is the opportunity to find a large group of coin dealers in one spot. It's as if your favorite mall had every hardware store in the city side by side. Say you collect Indian Head cents. There might be 10 or a dozen dealers who specialize in them. Can you hear opportunity knocking?

It's also a chance to meet and talk

to other collectors, at least some of who are probably interested in collecting the same things you are. At the larger shows there will be exhibits to learn from, club meetings, educational programs and even experts who can appraise or grade your coins.

Before you go, there are some things you need to know. Your first coin show is going to be a revelation in a lot of ways. If you know the rules beforehand, you will turn it into an exciting leap forward in the hobby.

First, make sure the show is going on as scheduled. Information about shows often is published months in advance. In the meantime, the show may have been postponed, moved or even cancelled. Nothing is more upsetting than driving to a coin show only to find an empty building. Even the big shows sometimes have problems.

For example, the 2005 ANA World's Fair of Money, the largest coin show in the world, had to be moved at the last minute from San Jose to San Francisco because of a conflicting event that was scheduled after the contracts had already been signed. The bigger shows will spread the word of any changes, but the smaller shows may not, so check ahead.

If you are planning on a distant show where you will be spending more than one day, most promoters will have a block of rooms at a nearby hotel at reduced rates. Find out and make reservations well in advance.

It's a good idea to take along a checklist of the coins you are looking for. Don't forget to bring a bag.

Q:
Can you quote the law used as the authority for ending 2-cent production?

A:
The 2-cent, and silver 3-cent coins died ignored. The Coinage Act of 1873 terminated the two denominations by not listing them as authorized coins.

Q:

I have a coin with extra incuse (and reversed) designs on both sides. How could that happen?

A:

You have a "sandwich" alteration. It was produced by sandwiching a coin between two others, then hammering the pile producing a coin which has incused, reversed images of the two outside coins in the pile. These are often mistaken for a double strike.

A heavy cloth shopping bag is a good starter. Later, you may want to get an aluminum case – like a small suitcase – or an attaché case to carry your coins. Vest-pocket dealers frequently use small, wheeled carry-on bags to carry their stock.

At many shows, there will be publications and other literature that will go in the bag. A price guide is also helpful, as is a notebook to keep track of your purchases and sales. You need to keep track for the IRS, as well as for your own records. A must is a business card or some other identification inside, for the unlikely event that you are separated from your bag.

You arrive at the front door of the show. Now what? Keep your wits about you as you look around. There are coins everywhere! At a small show, there may be only 20 to 30 dealers. At a large show, such as the Florida FUN Show, or the ANA World's Fair, there may be 500 or more dealers.

Depending on who is putting on the show, there will be a registration at the door, perhaps even a fee or an expected donation, or there may be an opportunity to participate in a door prize drawing. Coin shows have traditionally been free, but with rising costs more and more are charging an admission or a donation. This starts to bring them into line with other shows, such as gun shows, which have been charging fairly steep admissions for some time.

Entrance to a show is based on security. There are millions of dollars worth of coins on the dealer's tables, which they and the armed guards have to protect. You will probably need to wear a name or identification badge while you are in the show. If you try to walk in without one, you will be promptly sent back to get one.

The room where the dealers are set up is known as the "bourse" floor, a fancy French term for a room full of dealers. Everyone who comes to the show will follow their personal pattern, whether it's to stop at the first table, turn left, turn right or circle the room to see what's there before starting to seriously look at coins.

Here's where some rules come into play:

Don't walk up to a table and interrupt a transaction that is already going on. Wait your turn.

Ask, if you don't see the coin you are looking for on display, but remember, dealers specialize just like collectors, so you needn't bother to ask for a U.S. coins at a dealer's table displaying Roman coins.

Don't ever bring food or a drink with you to a dealer's table.

A spilled drink can do many thousands of dollars in damage that you could be liable for. The dealer may or may not caution you, but you can avoid embarrassment by closely following this advice.

Q:
I know there's a "tombstone" note, but was one of our coins referred to as the "tombstone" coin?

A:
While it was not a generally used nickname, some artistic circles charged the 2-cent coin with being "monumental art, engraved in the typical manner of a tombstone." I guess that would qualify it.

Q:

Are there any records to show how many of the U.S. half cents were melted down after they were withdrawn from circulation?

A:

Technically they are still in circulation, but Mint records show a total of less than $40 in face value is credited to melts of the denomination. The assumption is that they were lumped in with cent melts by weight.

Don't lay your bag (or anything else) on the glass display cases.

Besides the danger of breakage, you are hiding the dealer's stock from the next customer, in effect showing disrespect for the dealer's stock. This is also true at the tables offering free sample copies of hobby publications. I've manned the Krause table for years and I was always amazed by the frequent and callous disregard for common courtesy. If you are looking at several coins, or a box full, keep both hands (and the coins) above the table at all times.

If you are examining a dealer's stock, don't for any reason put coins in your lap.

They are out of sight of the dealer and set off alarm bells that might even result in your being asked to leave.

Don't mix your coins with the dealer's coins.

The dealer doesn't know you, so he is watching you because you just might be one of the thieves that show up at a lot of shows.

Keep the conversation at a minimum, unless the dealer encourages it.

A gushing and overly detailed description of every last coin in your collection is going to turn off the most patient of dealers. If you are the only customer, it's safe to ask questions, but as soon as another customer approaches, break it off. Show some courtesy and you may get invited back.

**Stay out of any deals going on around you.
Repeat: "Stay out."**

Don't pipe up and announce that there's a better example of the coin in another aisle or show one from your collection. Don't offer advice and don't try to outbid another buyer. Any kind of interference that might spoil a sale is going to get the dealer very angry, with good reason, so stay out.

Don't expect, or ask, for a "dealer" discount.

A couple of questions will expose the fact that you are lying. A dealer may give you a smaller discount, depending on the number of coins or value that you are buying. It doesn't hurt to bargain, but your success will vary from dealer to dealer, the time of day or how business is going.

Take time to look at the exhibits.

There is a tremendous amount of knowledge in a compact space that you can learn from.

Spend some time at any book dealer's table, looking for books on your specialty.

Remember, this is not a reading room or a library. Treat any book with care, especially soft cover books that will bend or fold easily. Both hard- and softcover books can suffer permanent damage if you open them too wide and break the back. Don't handle or touch books that you are not seriously interested in. Resist that temptation to "feel." If you have children with you,

Q:
I have a 1940 cent which has a one over the zero in the date. Is this a listed overdate?

A:
Your 1/0 in the date is damage to the 0 on a normal 1940 date cent. What frequently happens is that some sharp object shears the soft metal, shoving it into a ridge on top of the 0.

Q:

I have a 1903 dated Lincoln cent. Is this a pattern?

A:

You undoubtedly have an altered or counterfeit coin. There were no patterns for the Lincoln cent at that time.

impress on them and enforce the rule that they are not to touch anything without specific permission.

Another piece of advice has some ifs involved – it's usually never a good idea to spend all your money at one table. You may find a better example or a higher grade at another table, so sit firmly on your checkbook until you decide which is the best deal. On the other hand there's the Yard Sale Syndrome. If you don't buy it when you see it, the odds are it will be gone by the time you come back to the table – if you can find the table.

Having so many dealers gives you a much wider selection than what an individual dealer has to offer. Remember, dealers who offer coins for sale also buy coins. They have to, to stay in business. You may see only one or two "We Buy" signs, but if you have coins you want to sell, virtually every dealer whose specialty covers your coins will usually be ready to buy. Again, you can move from table to table for the best offer.

If a dealer turns his back to you, won't get his nose out of the newspaper, fails to greet you or ignores you in other ways, move on. He or she doesn't want your business and certainly won't offer you any bargains. If it were the only game in town you would be stuck with it, but at a coin show you have more options.

It all boils down to respect. If you treat a dealer and his stock in trade with respect, the dealer will treat you with the same respect. If not, move on to another table.

That's one of the nice things about a coin show. You have other chances to make a successful buy that will make your day.

For your first show, I'd recommend a lot of looking and not much buying. You are there to learn, rather than to collect. Watch how other collectors go about looking for their coins. Watch the dealers in action. As you get more shows under your belt, you will have a better idea of what's going on and how to spot any bargains that might tempt you. If you stick to the rules, things will go much easier for you and you will be able to more fully enjoy your visit to the bourse floor.

Coin club shows at any level have manpower problems. That's where you can fit in as a volunteer. You won't be alone. At a typical ANA national coin show there are several dozen jobs for volunteers. A local show may need 15 to 20 to help dealers set up and tear down, to sell tickets and memberships. As a volunteer you usually have some perks that make it worthwhile, so when your club is having a show, make sure your hand is up.

Select Coin Events

F.U.N.
Florida United Numismatists Annual Convention and Show
Early-January • Orlando, Florida

N.Y.I.N.C.
New York International Coin Convention
Mid-January
Manhattan, New York

Long Beach Coin Expo
Three Annual Shows
February, June & September
Long Beach, California

C.P.M.X.
Chicago Paper Money Expo
March • Chicago

Bay State Coin Show
Two Annual Shows
March & November • Boston

Baltimore Coin and Currency Convention
Three Annual Shows
March, July & December • Baltimore

Santa Clara Coin, Stamp & Collectibles Expo
Two Annual Shows
March & November
Santa Clara, California

C.I.C.F.
Chicago International Coin Fair
March-April • Chicago, Illinois

A.N.A.
American Numismatic Association
Spring Convention
Worlds Fair of Money in early August

S.N.A.
Garden State Numismatic Convention
May • New Jersey

Denver Coin Expo
May & September • Denver, Colorado

Memphis Paper Money Show
June • Memphis, Tennessee

C.D.A.
Professional Currency Dealers Association National Convention
November • St. Louis

M.S.N.S.
Michigan State Numismatic Society Fall Convention
November (Thanksgiving weekend)
Dearborn, Michigan

CHAPTER 57

TOKENS
AND MEDALS

The two items most often mislabeled as coins are tokens and medals, with good reason as both frequently have part of the characteristics of a coin.

Reviewing briefly, a coin is issued by a government body and assigned a specific value. A token is a privately issued piece that may have a denomination, but is backed only by the integrity of the issuing party. A medal has no denomination and is intended to celebrate some person, place or thing.

Tokens have played many roles in American history. The most prominent were the Civil War tokens issued by both sides, to alleviate a chronic coin shortage. They were widely used until several merchants refused to honor or redeem their tokens. The federal government stepped in and prohibited further production.

Perhaps most familiar are the legion of "good fors," tokens that bought a beer, a loaf of bread or a game of pool.

Both medals and tokens lack the exhaustive coverage that coins receive.

Because of the smaller number of collectors, there are fewer catalogs, price guides and other works, usually covering only a small fraction of the available pieces. The Token and Medal Society has done yeoman work in this area, as has the Civil War Token Society.

A few coins are noted for their artwork, but many if not most medals aptly demonstrate some of the finest talent in the field of numismatics. Because medals are mostly private issues, it is virtually impossible to get accurate mintage figures or other statistics needed by collectors. Artists are notoriously poor bookkeepers.

Q:

What was the purpose of the law passed in the early 1900s prohibiting the defacing of coins?

A:

The law was the direct outgrowth of the then current craze for love tokens. So many coins were being altered that the Treasury decided it needed a law to prohibit the practice, as well as the elongating of coins and making of coin jewelry. The law was rescinded in 1909 after most of the activity had stopped.

CHAPTER 58

COINS ON THE
INTERNET

For years, coin collectors have turned to printed price guides to value their coin collections. But with the advent of the Web, the latest market price updates are now available online.

NumisMaster.com, an online price guide powered by Krause Publications, debuted in late 2006. For a subscription fee, collectors can gain access to more than 1 million price listings. The entire Krause database of coin descriptions, values and images has been made available to the collecting public.

In addition, the site offers a collection management system, news, features, blogs, polls, show calendar and contests.

While many collectors still prefer thumbing through paper catalogs, the search function makes the online price guide easier to navigate. Say you have a coin with the date 1864 but you don't know what country it's from. NumisMaster allows you to view listings and photographs of every coin minted worldwide in 1864 making it much easier to make a match.

United States
Circulation Coinage

Cat#	Image	Denomination	Date(s)	Composition	Description	
KM# 25		Quarter	1796	0.892 Silver 0.1933 oz. ASW	**Name:** Draped Bust Quarter **Rev:** Small eagle	☑ View details ⊕ Add to portfolio
KM# 36		Quarter	1804–1807	0.892 Silver 0.1933 oz. ASW	**Name:** Draped Bust Quarter **Obv:** Draped bust right, flanked by stars, date at angle below **Rev:** Heraldic eagle	☑ View details ⊕ Add to portfolio
KM# 44		Quarter	1815–1828	0.892 Silver 0.1933 oz. ASW	**Name:** Liberty Cap Quarter **Obv:** Draped bust left, flanked by stars, date below **Rev:** Eagle with arrows in talons, banner above, value below	☑ View details ⊕ Add to portfolio
KM# 55		Quarter	1831–1838	0.892 Silver	**Name:** Liberty Cap Quarter **Obv:** Draped bust left, flanked by stars, date below **Rev:** Eagle with arrows in talons, value below	☑ View details ⊕ Add to portfolio
KM# 64.1		Quarter	1838–1840	0.9 Silver 0.1933 oz. ASW	**Name:** Seated Liberty Quarter **Obv:** Seated Liberty, stars around top 1/2 of border, date below **Rev:** Eagle with arrows in talons, value below	☑ View details ⊕ Add to portfolio
KM# 64.2		Quarter	1840–1853	0.9 Silver 0.1933 oz. ASW	**Name:** Seated Liberty Quarter **Obv:** Drapery added to Liberty's left elbow, stars around top 1/2 of border **Rev:** Eagle with arrows in talons, value below	☑ View details ⊕ Add to portfolio
KM# 78		Quarter	1853	0.9 Silver 0.18 oz. ASW	**Name:** Seated Liberty Quarter **Obv:** Seated Liberty, arrows at date **Rev:** Rays around eagle	☑ View details ⊕ Add to portfolio
KM# 81		Quarter	1854–1855	0.9 Silver 0.1933 oz. ASW	**Name:** Seated Liberty Quarter **Obv:** Seated Liberty, arrows at date **Rev:** Eagle with arrows in talons, value below	☑ View details ⊕ Add to portfolio
KM# A64.2					**Name:** Seated Liberty Quarter **Obv:** Seated Liberty, date below **Rev:** Eagle with arrows in	☑ View details ⊕ Add to portfolio
KM# 98						
KM# 106						
KM# A98						
KM# 114						
KM# 141						
KM# 145						
KM# 164						
KM# 164a						
KM# 204						

CHAPTER 59

THE
GLOSSARY

Way back at the beginning of this book, I mentioned the secret language of the coin collector. While I can't list all the terms and abbreviations, I've tried to list the most common ones. As you progress in the hobby you will find other terms and you will find other sources for their definitions.

First, a few common abbreviations:

AG: About Good; verbal coin grade

Ag: Scientific marking for silver

AGW: Actual Gold Weight in a coin

APW: Actual Platinum Weight in a coin

ASW: Actual Silver Weight in a coin

AU: About Uncirculated; adjectival coin grade

BU: Brilliant Uncirculated; adjectival coin grade

CAM, DCAM: Cameo, Deep Cameo

COA: Certificate of Authenticity

Cu: Scientific marking for copper

Cu-Ni: Scientific marking for copper-nickel alloy

— (Dash): In a chart means no figure available, especially mintage figures

DMPL: Deep Mirror Proof-like

Dwt: Pennyweight

EX (or XF): Extra Fine; adjectival coin grade

F: Fine; adjectival coin grade

Fe: Scientific marking for iron

FPL: Fixed Price List

G: Good; adjectival coin grade.

I.A. (Inc. Abv.); I.B. (Inc. Bel.): Included Above or Included Below; mintages of two or more varieties, or two or more years bulked together

MM: Mintmark

MS: Mint State or uncirculated; with a number (MS-60), a numerical grade

Ni: Scientific marking for nickel

OMM: Overmintmark; one letter over a different letter

PL: Proof-like

PVC: Polyvinyl Chloride

SASE: Self-Addressed Stamped Envelope

SMS: Special Mint Set (1965-1967)

V.D.B.: Initials on the reverse of a 1909 Lincoln cent.

TF: Tail Feathers, as 8TF on 1878 Morgan dollars.

Unc.: Uncirculated; adjectival coin grade

VF: Very Fine; adjectival coin grade

VG: Very Good; adjectival coin grade

XF (or EF): Extra Fine; adjectival coin grade

Zn: Scientific marking for zinc.

S-VDB
1909-S cent with Victor
David Brenner's initials

An 1878 Morgan dollar with eight tail feathers

Then come a few of the many numismatic terms:

Abrasion: Marks caused by friction or rubbing as a form of wear, as differing from bag marks or hairlines. Usually found on the high points of the design and not as deep or obvious as a contact mark.

Acid Date: A date, especially on a Buffalo nickel, made readable by applying acid to the coin. An alteration.

Alloy:
1. A mixture of two or more metals, melted and mixed together.
2. Referring to any metal or combination of metals mixed with bullion. Usually copper.

Alteration: Any deliberate change, such as the addition, removal or reworking of any design element on a coin, whether to deceive, confuse or to promote a cause. The so-called "Hobo" nickels are an exception, with some examples being quite valuable.

Average Circulated: Coin dealer term for a group of coins that generally grade at the low end of the grading scale, but for which there are no actual standards.

Avoirdupois Weight: Also known as merchant's weight. The commonly used weight in commerce — 16 ounces to a pound, etc. See Troy Weight.

Bourse: A hall or venue where dealers set up tables to display and buy and sell coins and other numismatic objects. From the French term for "exchange."

A chop-marked coin.

A coin with a large major die break. A "cud."

Chop Mark: Marks applied in the Orient to coins, indicating that they are full weight and the correct fineness. Found especially on the Mexican and U.S. Trade dollars.

Coin: A piece issued or sanctioned by a governmental body, with an assigned or stated commercial value.

Coin Folder: An open-face board with folds so that the outside protects the contents. Has holes for a given series or group of coins.

Collector Value (Numismatic Value): The amount above face value attached to a given coin because of its date, mintmark and grade.

Cud: (Slang) A fictional term for a major die break, so called because of the appearance of the raised metal as being similar to a "cud" of chewing gum or tobacco resting on the coin.

Die Break: A raised area of coin metal, above the normal surface, caused by the coin metal being forced into a hole left by a missing piece of the die face.

The 1983 and 1984 Olympic commemorative dollars had incuse dates

Die Crack: A raised line of coin metal, above the normal surface, caused by the coin metal being forced into a crack in the face of the die.

Face Value: The value of a coin as stated on the piece.

Incuse: The opposite of relief. A design that is sunk into the face of the coin or into the face of a die.

Key Coin: A coin that is one of the rarer grades, dates or mints for a given series.

Legend: The principal wording or phrase on a coin.

Machine Doubling Damage (MDD): Damage to a struck coin caused by one of the dies bouncing or chattering on the surface. The root cause is loose or worn parts of the machinery that allow slack that lets the die move about. The resulting doubling is often confused with Hub Doubling. Since this occurs after the final impact of the die pair, it is damaged and reduces rather than increases, collector value. Commonly mislabeled as Strike Doubling, Shift, Shift Doubling or Micro-Doubling.

Medal: A piece issued either by a government or a private entity intended to honor or memorialize a person, event, location or other worthy subject. Medals do not have a stated monetary value and are not intended for commerce. Often mislabeled as coins or tokens.

Minting Variety: A coin that is normal or exhibits a variation from the normal, as a result of any portion of the minting process, whether at the planchet stage, as a result of a change or modification of the die or during the striking process. It includes those classes considered to be intentional changes, as well as those caused by normal wear and tear on the dies or other minting equipment, and classes deemed to be "errors."

A planchet

Novelty Coin: Any coin that has been altered in some fashion after leaving the mint, including, but not limited to, cents with Lincoln smoking a pipe or cigar, with Kennedy's bust, with state maps, fraternal order symbols, etc. Technically an altered coin, but with minor collector value.

Overdate: Any date that has a second date with one or more differing digits superimposed by hubbing, punching or engraving the extra date.

Packaging Mistake: A mint-packaged proof or mint set that has a missing coin, duplicate coins, two coins in one hole or partition or any other mistake.

Slabbed Coins

Planchet: The processed disc (usually metal) that is placed between the die pair to be struck as a coin.

Proof-like: A coin that exhibits some, but not all of the characteristics of a proof coin, such as mirror fields, sharp strike (two or more), frosted devices, etc.

Ringing an Auction: Collusion between several buyers eliminating competition by agreeing in advance on what items they will bid for.

Ring Test: A negative test involving dropping the coin on a hard surface to determine the metal content by the sound, or "ring" of the coin. The smallest internal defect or void will cause a perfectly good bullion coin to sound like a block of lead.

Sea Salvage (Water Damage): Term used to describe coins recovered from ocean wrecks. The coins usually show damage from long contact with salt water, or with the sand, affecting silver coins more than the gold.

Shotgun Roll: (Slang) A paper roll with both ends crimped, similar to the end of a shotgun shell, hence the name. The method of rolling exposes most of the two end coins.

Slab, Slabbing, Slabbed: (Slang) A hard plastic case used by a third-party grading service to encapsulate a coin that has been graded and authenticated.

Token: A privately issued piece, usually with an assigned value intended for use similar to a coin.

Troy Weight: A system of weights used primarily for bullion, in which 12 Troy ounces equal one Troy pound, or 5,760 grains. A troy ounce equals 480 grains or 31.103 grams. (See Avoirdupois Weight)

TRVST on a
Peace dollar.

Q:
Which was the "Ship on wheels" commemorative?

A:
This was a slighting reference to the design of the 1892-93 Columbian Expo half. The reverse has a ship above two globes, which resemble wheels.

TRVST: The spelling of TRUST on all Peace dollars and Standing Liberty quarters. The cause is blamed on artistic license based on the lack of a U in the Roman alphabet.

Whiz, Whizzing: To alter the surface of a coin by removing or moving the surface metal about. A practice condemned by the ANA and the Professional Numismatist's Guild.

Wooden Money: Properly tokens, printed on pieces of wood. The first were on thin slices of wood. Later rounds similar to coins also were used. Some medals are found that are actually struck on wood.

CHAPTER 60

The
ANA
Grading Guide

With permission from the American Numismatic Association (ANA), I am including an excerpt from the official ANA Grading Guide to help you to better understand the grading terms and their meaning. A basic understanding of how to grade your coins is vital to your collecting interests at any level. Grades listed are based on the following standards established by the American Numismatic Association.

For more detailed descriptions, see the *Official ANA Grading Standards for United States Coins*, by Ken Bressett and A. Kosoff (American Numismatic Association, 818 N. Cascade Ave., Colorado Springs, CO 80903-3279). The Web address is www.money.org.

Proof Coins

The term "proof" refers to a manufacturing process that results in a special surface or finish on coins made for collectors. Most familiar are modern brilliant proofs. These coins are struck at the U.S. Mint by a special process. Carefully prepared dies, sharp in all features, are made. Then the flat surfaces of the dies are given a high, mirror-like polish. Specially prepared planchets are fed into low-speed coining presses. Each proof coin is slowly and carefully struck more than once to accentuate details. When striking is completed, the coin is taken from the dies with care and not allowed to come in contact with other pieces. The result is a coin with a mirror-like surface.

From 1817 through 1857, proof coins were made only on special occasions and not for general sale to collectors. They were made available to visiting foreign dignitaries, government officials and those with connections at the Mint. Earlier (pre-1817) U.S. coins may have proof-like surfaces and many proof characteristics (1796 silver coins are good examples), but they were not specifically or intentionally struck as proofs. These are sometimes designated as "specimen strikings."

Beginning in 1858, proofs were sold to collectors openly. In that year, 80 silver proof sets (containing silver coins from the 3-cent through the dollar), plus additional pieces of the silver dollar denomination were produced, as well as approximately 200 (the exact number is not known) copper-nickel cents and a limited number of proof gold coins.

The traditional, or "brilliant," type of proof finish was used on all American proof coins of the 19th century. During the 20th century, cents through the 1909 Indian type, nickels

Q:
Did the Canadian Royal Mint strike Trade dollars intended for jewelry?

A:
If you are referring to the pieces that have the wording "FOR JEWELRY" rather than "ONE DOLLAR," the answer is definitely no. These are Chinese counterfeits, intended to bilk the illiterate.

Q:

Has the United States ever struck coins denominated in pesos?

A:

Careful before you jump on this one. All of the peso denominated coins used in the Philippines between 1903 and 1947 were struck either at the U.S. mainland mints or the U.S. Branch Mint in Manila.

through the 1912 Liberty, regular-issue silver coins through 1915 and gold coins through 1907 were of the brilliant type. When modern proof coinage was resumed in 1936 and continued through 1942, then 1950-1964, and 1968 to date, the brilliant finish was used. These types of proofs are referred to as "brilliant proofs," although actual specimens may have toned over the years. The mirror-like surface is still evident, however.

From 1908 through 1915, matte proofs and sandblast proofs (the latter made by directing fine sand particles at high pressure toward the coin's surface) were made of certain coins. Exceptions are the 1909-1910 proofs with Roman finish. Characteristics vary from issue to issue, but generally all of these pieces have extreme sharpness of design detail and sharp, squared-off rims. The surfaces are without luster and have a dullish matte surface. Sandblasted proofs were made of certain commemoratives also, such as the 1928 Hawaiian issue.

Roman-finish proof gold coins were made in 1909 and 1910. These pieces are sharply struck and have squared-off edges and a satin-like surface finish, not too much different from an uncirculated coin (which causes confusion among collectors today and which, at the time of issue, was quite unpopular because collectors resented having to pay a premium for a coin without a distinctly different appearance).

Matte proofs were made of 1908-1917 Lincoln cents and 1913-1917 Buffalo nickels. Such coins have extremely sharp design detail, squared-off rims, and "brilliant" (mirror-like) edges, but a matte or satin-like (or even satin surface, not with flashy mint luster) surface. In some instances, matte proof dies may have been used to make regular circulation strikes once the requisite number of matte proofs was made for collectors. So it is important that a matte proof, to be considered authentic, have squared-off rims and mirror-like perfect edges in addition to the proper surface characteristics.

Additional points concerning proofs: Certain regular issues, or business strikes, have nearly full proof-like surfaces. These were produced in several ways. Usually regular-issue dies (intended to make coins for circulation) were polished to remove surface marks or defects for extended use. Coins struck from these dies were produced at high speed, and the full proof surface is not always evident. Also, the pieces are struck on ordinary planchets. Usually such pieces, sometimes called "first strikes" or "proof-like uncirculated," have patches of uncirculated mint frost.

A characteristic in this regard is the shield on the reverse (on coins with this design feature). The stripes within the shield on proofs are fully brilliant, but on proof-like non-proofs the stripes usually are not mirror-like. Also, the striking may by weak in areas and the rims might not be sharp.

The mirror-like surface of a brilliant proof coin is much more susceptible to damage than the surfaces of an uncirculated coin. For this reason, proof coins that have been cleaned often show a series of fine hairlines or minute striations. Also, careless handling has resulted in certain proofs acquiring marks, nicks and scratches.

Some proofs, particularly 19th-century issues, have "lint marks." When a proof die was wiped with an oily rag, sometimes threads, bits of hair, lint and so on would remain. When a coin was struck from such a die, an incuse or recess impression of the debris would appear on the piece. Lint marks visible to the unaided eye should be specially mentioned in a description.

Q:

Coins have a long life expectancy, but wasn't there an unusual period estimated for the steel cents?

A:

When the 1943 zinc plated steel cents went into circulation, Moses E. Smith, Superintendent of the Denver Mint is quoted as stating, "Steel pennies (sic) will probably be in circulation for the next 100 years." This ranks with President Johnson's statement that silver coins would remain in circulation alongside the clad coins in 1965.

Proofs are divided into the following classifications:

Proof-70: "perfect proof," has no hairlines, handling marks or other defects; in other words, a flawless coin. Such a coin may be brilliant or may have natural toning.

Proof-67: A grade midway between Proof-70 and Proof-65 and would be noticeably finer than Proof-65.

Proof-65: "Choice proof," refers to a proof that may show some very fine hairlines, usually from friction-type cleaning or friction-type drying or rubbing after dipping. To the unaided eye, a Proof-65 will appear to be virtually perfect. However, 4X magnification will reveal some minute lines. Such hairlines are best seen under strong incandescent light.

Proof-63: A coin midway between Proof-65 and Proof-60.

Proof-60: A coin with some scattered handling marks and hairlines visible to the unaided eye.

Impaired proofs and other comments: If a proof has been excessively cleaned, has many marks, scratches, dents or other defects, it is described as an impaired proof. If the coin has seen extensive wear, then it will be graded one of the lesser grades: Proof-55, Proof-45, and so on.

It is not logical to describe a slightly worn proof as "AU" ("almost uncirculated") for it never was "uncirculated" in the sense that uncirculated describes a top-grade, normal-production strike. So the term "impaired proof" is appropriate. It is best to describe fully such a coin.

Examples: "Proof with extensive hairlines and scuffing." "Proof with numerous nicks and scratches in the field." "Proof-55, with light wear on the higher surfaces."

UNCIRCULATED COINS:

Uncirculated coins: The term "uncirculated," interchangeable with "mint state," refers to a coin that has never seen circulation. Such a piece has no wear of any kind. A coin as bright as the time it was minted or with very light natural toning can be described as "toned uncirculated."

Except for copper coins, the presence or absence of light toning does not effect an uncirculated coin's grade. Indeed, among silver coins, attractive natural toning often results in the coin bringing a premium. The quality of luster or "mint bloom" on an uncirculated coin is an essential element in correctly grading the piece and has a bearing on its value. Luster may in time become dull, frosty, spotted, or discolored. Unattractive luster will normally lower the grade.

Except for certain special mint sets made in recent years for collectors, uncirculated, or normal production-strike coins, were produced on high-speed presses, stored in bags together with other coins, run through counting machines, and in other ways handled without regard to numismatic posterity. As a result, it is the rule and not the exception for an uncirculated coin to have bag marks and evidence of coin-to-coin contact, although the piece might not have seen actual commercial circulation. The number of such marks will depend on the coin's size.

Differences in criteria in this regard are given in the individual sections under grading descriptions for different denominations and types.

Uncirculated coins can be divided into five major categories:

MS-70: "Perfect uncirculated," the finest quality available. Such a coin under 4X magnification will show no bag marks, lines, or other evidence of handling or contact with other coins. A brilliant coin may be described as "MS-70 brilliant" or "perfect brilliant uncirculated." A lightly toned nickel or silver coin may be described as "MS-70 toned" or "perfect toned uncirculated." Or, in the cases of particularly attractive or unusual toning, additional adjectives may be in order such as "perfect uncirculated with attractive iridescent toning around the borders."

To qualify as MS-70, a copper or bronze coin must have its full luster and natural surface color, and may not be toned brown, olive, or any other color. Coins with toned surfaces that are otherwise perfect should be described as MS-65, rather than MS-67.

MS-60: A coin between MS-70 and MS-65. The coin may be either brilliant or toned (except for a copper coin, for which a toned piece should be described as MS-65).

MS-65: This refers to an above uncirculated coin that may be brilliant or toned (and described accordingly) and that has fewer bag marks than usual; scattered, occasional bag marks on the surface or perhaps one or two very light rim marks.

MS-63: A coin midway between MS-65 and MS-60.

MS-60: Uncirculated (typical uncirculated without any other adjectives) refers to a coin that has a moderate number of bag marks on its surface. Also present may be a few minor edge nicks and marks, although not of a serious nature. Unusually deep bag marks, nicks and the like must be described separately. A coin may be either brilliant or toned.

Grading standard interpretations: The official ANA grading standards in the mint-state range as described have been adapted in assigning the market valuations presented for U.S. issues, to conform to consensus interpretations prevailing in the marketplace.

The numerical grades, along with their prevailing adjectival grades and descriptions, are as follows:

MS-63: (choice uncirculated) Choice quality specimens with minimal weaknesses or blemish readily evident.

MS-64: Choice quality specimens with eye appeal and only the smallest distracting weakness, blemish or bag marks.

MS-65: (gem uncirculated) Sharply struck, hairline-free coins with full luster and no distracting blemishes.

MS-67: Described as "gem" according to official ANA criteria, it is not presently associated with an adjectival equivalent. There is also not a consensus description that is associated with this grade.

Striking and mint peculiarities on uncirculated coins: Certain early U.S. gold and silver coins have mint-caused planchet or adjustment marks, a series of parallel striations. If these are visible to the naked eye, they should be described adjectively in addition to the numerical or regular descriptive grade.

Examples: "MS-60 with adjustment marks," or "MS-65 with adjustment marks," or "perfect uncirculated with very light adjustment marks," etc.

If an uncirculated coin exhibits weakness due to striking or die wear, or unusual (for the variety) die wear, this must be adjectively mentioned in addition to the grade.

Examples: "MS-60 lightly struck" or "choice uncirculated, lightly struck," and "MS-70, lightly struck."

CIRCULATED COINS:

Once a coin enters circulation, it begins to show signs of wear. As time goes on, the coin becomes more and more worn until, after a period of many decades, only a few features may be left.

Dr. William H. Sheldon devised a numerical scale to indicate degrees of wear. According to this scale, a coin in condition 1, or "basal state," is barely recognizable. At the opposite end, a coin touched by even the slightest trace of wear (below MS-60) cannot be called uncirculated.

Although numbers from 1 through 59 are continuous, it has been found practical to designate specific intermediate numbers to define grades. Hence, this text uses the following descriptions and their numerical equivalents:

ABOUT UNCIRCULATED

AU-50 (about uncirculated): Just a slight amount of wear from brief exposure to circulation or light rubbing from mishandling may be found on the elevated design areas. Those imperfections may appear as scratches or dull spots, along with bag marks or edge nicks. At least half of the original mint luster will usually be present.

The pictures demonstrate the various grades on representative denominations.

Indian Cent

Lincoln Cent

 **Buffalo Nickel**

Jefferson Nickel

 **Mercury Dime**

ABOUT UNCIRCULATED

Standing Liberty Quarter

Washington Quarter

Walking Liberty Half

Morgan Dollar

Barber Coins

EXTREMELY FINE

Indian Cent

Lincoln Cent

Buffalo Nickel

Jefferson Nickel

Mercury Dime

EXTREMELY FINE

Standing Liberty Quarter

Washington Quarter

Walking Liberty Half

Morgan Dollar

Barber Coins

VERY FINE

VF-20 (very fine): Coins reflect noticeable wear at the fine points in the design, though they may remain sharp overall. Although the details will be slightly smoothed, all lettering and major features must remain sharp.

Indian cent: All letters in LIBERTY complete but worn; headdress shows considerable flatness, with flat spots on tips of feathers.

Lincoln cent: Hair, cheek, jaw and bow-tie details will be worn but clearly separated, and wheat stalks on the reverse will be full, with no weak spots.

Buffalo nickel: High spots on hair braid and cheek will be flat but show more detail, and a full horn will remain on the buffalo.

Jefferson nickel: Well over half of the major hair detail will remain, and the pillars on Monticello will remain well defined, with triangular roof partially visible.

Mercury dime: Hair braid will show some detail, and three-quarters of the details will remain in the feathers. The two diagonal bands on the fasces will show completely, but be worn smooth at the middle, with the vertical lines sharp.

VERY FINE

Standing Liberty quarter:
Rounded contour of Liberty's right leg will be flattened, as will high point of shield.

Washington Quarter

Walking Liberty half dollar: All lines of the skirt will show but be worn on high points, and over half of the feathers will show on eagle.

Morgan dollar: Two-thirds of hairlines rom forehead to ear must show, and ear will be well defined, while feathers on eagle's breast may be worn smooth.

Barber coins: All seven letters of "LIBERTY" on headband must stand out sharply, while head wreath will be well outlined top to bottom.

FINE

F-12 (fine): This is the most widely collected condition. Coins show evidence of moderate to considerable but generally even wear on all high points, though all elements of the design and lettering remain bold. Where LIBERTY appears on the headband it must be fully visible. The rim must be fully raised and sharp on 20th century coins.

Indian Cent

Buffalo Nickel

Lincoln Cent

Jefferson Nickel

Mercury Dime

FINE

Standing Liberty Quarter

Washington Quarter

Walking Liberty Half Dollar

Morgan Dollar

Barber Coins

VERY GOOD

VG-8 (very good): Coins show considerable wear, with most of the points of detail worn nearly smooth. At least three letters must show where LIBERTY appears in a headband. On 20th-century coinage, the rim is starting to merge with the lettering.

Indian Cent

Lincoln Cent

 **Buffalo Nickel**

Jefferson Nickel

 **Mercury Dime**

VERY GOOD

Standing Liberty Quarter

Washington Quarter

Walking Liberty Half Dollar

Morgan Dollar

Barber Coins

GOOD

G-4 (good): In this condition, only the basic design detail remains distinguishable in outline form, with all points of detail being worn smooth. LIBERTY has disappeared and rims are nearly merging with the lettering.

Indian Cent

Lincoln Cent

Buffalo Nickel

Jefferson Nickel

Mercury Dime

GOOD

Standing Liberty Quarter

Washington Quarter

Walking Liberty Half Dollar

Morgan Dollar

Barber Coins

SOME NOTES

Good or Fair: A coin identifiable by date and mint but otherwise badly worn, with only parts of the lettering showing. Such coins are of value to collectors only as space fillers and command a significant premium only in cases of extreme scarcity.

Proof: Created as collector coins, proof specimens are struck on specially selected planchets with highly polished dies and generally display a mirrorlike finish, sometimes featuring frosted highlight areas.

Prooflike and deep-mirror prooflike (DMPL): These terms describe the degree of reflectiveness and cameo contrast on well-struck Morgan dollars. A DMPL coin may appear to be a proof at first glance, and a prooflike specimen has a lesser (but still considerable) degree of flash. Bag marks are more noticeable on PL and DMPL Morgans. Some common dates are scarce in this condition.

Note: The exact description of circulated grades varies widely from issue to issue, so the preceding is a general summary only. For a more detailed description of the grades and grading methods, purchase the latest edition of the *Official ANA Grading Standards for United States Coins* by the American Numismatic Association.

EPILOGUE

This is the end. I hope that you won't put this book away and never open it again. This book should be consulted on a frequent basis. There are pieces of advice that you may need to be reminded of or ideas that you want to follow up on. If you have questions, by all means get in touch with me and I'll be glad to help.

CONTACT ADDRESSES

Alan Herbert: AnswerMan2@aol.com

F+W Media NumisMaster: www.NumisMaster.com

Catalogs: www.shopNumisMaster.com

Bank Note Reporter: www.BankNoteReporter.com

Coin Prices, Coins Magazine: www.NumisMaster.com

Numismatic News: www.NumismaticNews.com

World Coin News: www.WorldCoinNews.net

United States coins are often given nicknames based on their obverse design. This Type Identification Guide is a start for coin identification. It also shows the changes in the sizes of various denominations over time.

Half Cent

LIBERTY CAP
Year Struck: 1793

*For more on the
Half Cent, see
Chapter 23, page 96*

LIBERTY CAP
Years Struck: 1794-1797

DRAPED BUST
Years Struck: 1800-1808

CLASSIC HEAD
Years Struck: 1809-1836

BRAIDED HAIR
Years Struck: 1840-1857

Large Cent

FLOWING HAIR
Year Struck: 1793

LIBERTY CAP
Years Struck: 1793-1796

DRAPED BUST
Years Struck: 1796-1807

CLASSIC HEAD
Years Struck: 1808-1814

*For more on the
Large Cent, see
Chapter 24, page 98*

CORONET
Years Struck: 1816-1839

BRAIDED HAIR
Years Struck: 1840-1857

Small Cent

FLYING EAGLE
Years Struck: 1856-1858

INDIAN HEAD
Years Struck: 1859-1909

LINCOLN
Years Struck: 1909-date

*For more on the
Small Cent, see
Chapter 24, page 98*

SHIELD 2-CENT
Years Struck: 1864-1873

SILVER 3 CENTS
Years Struck: 1851-1873

CORONET
COPPER-NICKEL 3-CENT
Years Struck: 1865-1889

HALF DIME

FLOWING HAIR
Years Struck: 1794-1795

DRAPED BUST
Years Struck: 1796-1805

LIBERTY CAP

Years Struck: 1829-1837

For more on the Half Dime, see Chapter 27, page 104

SEATED LIBERTY

Years Struck: 1837-1873

NICKEL

SHIELD
Years Struck: 1866-1883

LIBERTY
Years Struck: 1883-1913

BUFFALO
Years Struck: 1913-1938

JEFFERSON
Years Struck: 1938-2004

For more on the Nickel, see Chapter 28, page 106

JEFFERSON
LARGE PROFILE
Year Struck: 2005

JEFFERSON
LARGE FACING PORTRAIT
Years Struck: 2006-date

Twenty Cents

For more on the Twenty Cent coin, see Chapter 30, page 112

SEATED LIBERTY
WITHIN CIRCLE OF STARS
Years Struck: 1875-1878

QUARTER

DRAPED BUST
Years Struck: 1796-1807

For more on Quarters, see Chapters 31-33, starting on page 114

LIBERTY CAP
Years Struck: 1815-1838

SEATED LIBERTY
Years Struck: 1838-1891

QUARTER

BARBER
Years Struck: 1892-1916

STANDING LIBERTY
Years Struck: 1916-1930

WASHINGTON
Years Struck: 1932-1998

50 STATE

Years Struck: 1999-2008

For more on Quarters, see Chapters 31-33, starting on page 114

TERRITORIAL

Year Struck: 2009

AMERICA THE BEAUTIFUL

Years Struck: 2010-date

HALF DOLLAR

FLOWING HAIR
Years Struck: 1794-1795

DRAPED BUST
Years Struck: 1796-1807

CAPPED BUST
Years Struck: 1807-1839

SEATED LIBERTY
Years Struck: 1839-1891

BARBER

Years Struck: 1892-1915

*For more on the
Half Dollar coin,
see Chapter 34,
page 136*

WALKING LIBERTY

Years Struck: 1916-1947

FRANKLIN

Years Struck: 1948-1963

KENNEDY

Years Struck: 1964-date

DOLLAR

FLOWING HAIR
Years Struck: 1794-1795

DRAPED BUST
Years Struck: 1795-1803

For more on the Dollar coin, see Chapters 35-44, starting on page 140

GOBRECHT

Years Struck: 1836-1839

SEATED LIBERTY

Years Struck: 1840-1873

DOLLAR

TRADE

Years Struck: 1873-1885

MORGAN

Years Struck: 1878-1921

For more on the Dollar coin, see Chapters 35-44, starting on page 140

PEACE

Years Struck: 1921-1935

EISENHOWER

Years Struck: 1971-1978

DOLLAR

For more on the Dollar coin, see Chapters 35-44, starting on page 140

SUSAN B. ANTHONY
Years Struck: 1979-1999

SACAGAWEA
Years Struck: 2000-date

PRESIDENTS
Year Struck: 2007

Gold Dollar

For more on the
Gold Dollar coin,
see Chapter 43,
page 164

LIBERTY HEAD-TYPE 1
Years Struck: 1849-1854

INDIAN HEAD-TYPE 2
Years Struck: 1854-1856

INDIAN HEAD-TYPE 3
Years Struck: 1856-1889

$2.50 GOLD QUARTER EAGLE

LIBERTY CAP
Years Struck: 1796-1807

TURBAN HEAD
Year Struck: 1808

TURBAN HEAD
Years Struck: 1821-1834

CLASSIC HEAD

Years Struck: 1834-1839

For more on the $2.50 Gold Quarter Eagle, see Chapter 45, page 166

CORONET HEAD

Years Struck: 1840-1907

INDIAN HEAD

Years Struck: 1908-1929

$3 Gold

For more on the $3 Gold coin, see Chapter 46, page 167

INDIAN HEAD WITH HEADDRESS

Years Struck: 1854-1889

ABOUT THE $3 GOLD

It was a federal partnership of sorts.

The $3 gold coin was struck from 1854 to 1889 with the Postal Service in mind.

When the coin was first introduced, a first class stamp was worth 3 cents, and they were often sold in sheets of 100. A $3 coin would be just the right amount to buy a sheet of stamps.

Unfortunately, the plan never really took off and mintages for the coin were low throughout the series.

$5 Gold Half Eagle

LIBERTY CAP

Years Struck: 1795-1807

TURBAN HEAD

Years Struck: 1807-1834

CLASSIC HEAD

Years Struck: 1834-1838

CORONET HEAD

Years Struck: 1839-1908

For more on the $5 Gold Half Eagle, see Chapter 47, page 168

INDIAN HEAD

Years Struck: 1908-1929

$10 Gold Eagle

For more on the $10 Gold Half Eagle, see Chapter 48, page 170

LIBERTY CAP

Years Struck: 1795-1804

CORONET HEAD

Years Struck: 1838-1907

INDIAN HEAD

Years Struck: 1907-1933

$20 Gold Double Eagle

CORONET HEAD

Years Struck: 1849-1907

For more on the $20 Gold Half Eagle, see Chapter 49, page 172

SAINT-GAUDENS

Years Struck: 1907-1933

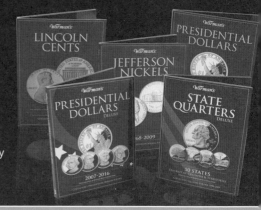

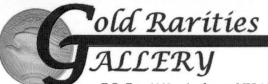